In the Chinese Kitchen
with
Shirley Fong-Torres

Pacific View Press
Berkeley, California

Cover photo by Post Street Portraits, San Francisco

Cover design by Cecilia Brunazzi

Text design by Linda Revel

Library of Congress Catalog Card Number: 92-83782

ISBN 1-881896-03-X

Printed in the United States of America

*This book is dedicated
to my family*

About the Author

Shirley Fong-Torres grew up in Oakland, California, where her parents operated Chinese restaurants. After her graduation from the University of California at Berkeley, she taught junior high and high school in Texas and California. She worked for Levi-Strauss for eight years, where her last position was operations manager of women's wear merchandising. Her love of Chinese cooking and her interest in Chinese-American history eventually merged, resulting in her leaving the corporate world to form her two companies: Wok Wiz Chinatown Tours & Cooking Company and A Taste of Chinatown.

Shirley's articles on Chinese food and her restaurant reviews appear regularly in local and national publications, and she is a popular guest chef on radio and television.

She has served on the Board of Directors of the San Francisco Convention and Visitors Bureau and is active with numerous other community and Asian-American business, civic, and food professional groups. She still found time to write two previous books, *San Francisco Chinatown: A Walking Tour* and *Wok Wiz Chinatown Tour Cookbook.* She lives near San Francisco with her husband, Bernard Carver and her daughter, Tina Dong.

For more information about Shirley's walking tours and cooking programs, contact Wok Wiz Chinatown Tours and Cooking Company, 750 Kearny Street, Suite 800, San Francisco, CA 94108, or call 415-355-9657.

Contents

Acknowledgments

Putting together a book takes time, effort, patience, and a boundless supply of energy. With the help and support of numerous friends and colleagues, and especially a loving family, this task was made easier. My third book was written with the encouragement of these important people in my life, and I wish to say thank you to one and all.

Thank you to editor and publishers, Bob Schildgen, Nancy Ippolito, and Pam Zumwalt, who kept me busy on this book. To Robbi Ernst of Post Street Portraits; a trio of top photographers, Tony Baroque, Frank Cimo, and Rob Werfel; hair stylist Deborah Albanese; Pat and John Vogel for the use of their beautiful kitchen for my television shows and this cookbook cover; to Lee Hinton, my video producer who spends hours upon hours with me in Chinatown or taping my cooking and walking tour programs.

It is an honor to associate with professionals who have become my friends, who I can call on for advice, and as busy as they are, who give so generously of their assistance. Over the years, I have cultivated friendships with many people in the food and wine industry, and I believe that we learn from one another. I am proud to know and work with famed chefs and authors Martin Yan, Ken Hom, food editor John Doerper, publishers Ray and Barbara March, and Sonoma County's Viansa Winery representative Ron Mangini—I celebrate your successes and appreciate your friendship. Lisa Somogyi and Rodger Helwig were kind to share Roederer Estate champagne, Rodney Strong, and Davis Bynum wines for my wine-and-Chinese-food pairings. Phil Watson proved that Ginger Flavored Currant Wine is excellent to use in Chinese cooking. A special hug to Joyce Chen in Boston, who voiced her belief in me with words of wisdom, when we first met in 1984, long before the Wok Wiz company emerged.

My Wok Wiz walking tour business blossomed due in large to a loyal and professional staff. I love to do these tours, but cannot conduct them all by myself. I rely on this incomparable team: Larry Mak, a part-time actor; Dorothy Quock, a "save the precious panda" campaigner; bubbly and delightful June Lee; cheerful Ophelia Wong; Chinatown natives George Mew, Martha Mew, Bernice Fong, Howard Teng (great story teller, Howard!); chef and budding cookbook author/performer Hank Quock, Chinese food expert Rhoda Wing, and the newest member of our staff, Irene Fong. In my home office, Madeline Sherry continues to keep me organized because she is so thorough and detail-oriented. I love the early-morning telephone chats with Alcatraz's most famous former guard, Frank Heaney, and Frisco Tours' Mark Gordon—we are all busy, so 7 a.m. is a swell time to talk! Thanks to my eating staff, my comrades with chopsticks always poised and ready: Angie and Ray Campodonico, Joyce and Brian Narlock—we never grow tired of eating fine Chinese meals, do we? Wil and Lorraine Lew spent countless hours testing my recipes, and gave me some good ideas, as did my father-in-law Bernard Carver, who lives in Springfield, Illinois.

To all my friends, especially the ones from college and the 1980s Levi Strauss & Co. days: my new career has kept us apart—I promise to try harder to make more time for play.

A bouquet of kisses for my tireless husband, Bernie Carver—your love, unfailing loyalty, patience, and kind heart feed my energetic outlook and zest for life; to my daughter Tina Dong, ever so helpful in the kitchen and office, and always so thoughtful a young lady; to Father, a retired restaurateur, and Mother, thank you for sitting with me to tell stories about Chinese recipes and remind me of times shared in the family kitchen. I appreciate the outspoken as well as unspoken support from my sister Sarah and her husband Dave; my brothers Ben and Burt and their wives, Dianne and Cindy; my niece Lea, my nephew Jason. And I owe much to the memory of our brother Barry, and my mother-in-law Rose. Both of you are in my heart and thoughts every day.

To the staff of Wheel of Fortune, especially Merv Griffin, Suzy Rosenberg, and Nancy Jones—you know how grateful I am to have been selected as a contestant on your famous television game show, as my life has not been quite the same since that appearance in 1987. Last but not least, wokfuls of thank yous to the thousands of visitors who have come to share adventures in Chinatown on our walking tours, and to the other thousands of cooking students from near and far, since 1973 when I started teaching, to the present. You prove to me class after class and year after year that food brings people together for immense joy in life. May your hearts and woks always brim with goodness.

Introduction

 hinese cooking is probably the most socially oriented in the world. To be enjoyed to the fullest, Chinese food should be shared, and it is difficult to eat it alone. Many foods have special symbolic meanings that reinforce social ties, and eating together is considered an expression of love and respect from the cook to those who share the meal. The experience of delicious food nourishes the body and the spirit.

For the Chinese, food has always played a major role in daily life. When families and friends get together, they eat. Chinese festivals and holidays are always preoccupied with food and its meaning, with a great deal of tradition and folklore involved. For example, long noodles are frequently served at birthday celebrations to insure longevity. When fish is presented, it isn't just fish, but has a double meaning, because the word for fish in Cantonese sounds like "abundance" and "easy-going." At New Year's dining, the fish is cooked without being cut up, to represent unity. To celebrate the arrival of autumn, on the 15th day of the 8th month of the lunar calendar, we give and receive boxes of mooncakes. The egg yolk in the center of the cakes represents the moon. The most precious and expensive mooncakes have double yolks. Chinese people who believe in an afterlife set up religious altars where the deceased person's favorite foods are placed for his or her spiritual consumption.

My childhood memories center around life at our family restaurants in Oakland, California, and in particular, the Bamboo Hut in nearby Hayward. My father operated two restaurants in our hometown of Oakland, and one each in Hayward, Reno, Nevada, and Amarillo, Texas. He was a chef at world famous Trader Vic's restaurant for two years. When I was a little girl, I spent most of the time after classes at Lincoln Elementary School and before late afternoon Chinese language school in the kitchen or back rooms of our family's New Eastern Cafe in Oakland. I recall waking up from afternoon naps on a cot next to 100-pound bags of rice piled high in the supply room. The scent of raw rice and vision of playing on the bags is still very vivid. Coincidentally, *The Rice Room* is the title of my brother Ben's second book, a memoir about growing up in Oakland's Chinatown. It was in that rice room area that our eldest sister Sarah taught my brothers and me how to jitterbug to radio music.

Our father and my eldest brother Barry left California briefly in 1955 to start a restaurant in Reno, and in 1957 Dad and Ben traveled to Amarillo to launch the Ding How restaurant. On December 2, 1961, the Bamboo Hut opened its doors. I stumbled through those years, entering high school and college, falling in love and "rocking out" with the Beatles and Rolling Stones along with the rest of the teenagers of our time. Unlike my friends, though, I took an hour-long bus ride every day from Oakland High School to work at our Bamboo Hut. It was there, during my formative teen years, that I learned so much. Along with my brothers, I must have peeled thousands of prawns, wrapped endless won tons, egg rolls, and packaged paper-wrapped chicken. I was at Dad's side to learn how to make gravies and sauces. We instinctively honed our skills with customer service by waiting on tables. Years were to pass before I came to fully appreciate the knowledge of food and people my parents instilled in us.

Every evening at the Bamboo Hut our family dined together in one of the back booths, always late, after the dinner rush was over. The meal usually consisted of a clear soup, a simple vegetable, steamed pork or chicken, always healthy food. For special treats, we had Dad's crisp fried chicken or fried prawns. Occasionally, Mom or Dad prepared an herbal soup, which we drank obediently. I believe our overall good health is a result of the many soups we consumed.

Dad retired from the restaurant business in 1973, the same year I started to teach Chinese cooking in Pacifica, California. Then it was a hobby, an enjoyable diversion, and a way to carry on my father's legacy. Almost 20 years later, I continue to teach Chinese cooking, but now travel throughout the world to share my joy of cooking both northern- and southern-style Chinese food.

Food and people together, always so important to me, became an integral part of my business life, through a twist of fate in 1987. With the encouragement of my Chinese cooking class students, I tried out for the popular game show, Wheel of Fortune, and became one of the four contestants chosen out of a group of 200. At that time, I was a single parent who had only recently left the corporate world of Levi Strauss & Company to pursue the dream of running my own business. Although I did not win much, the appearance on national television on February 18, 1987 gave a wonderful boost to my new Chinatown walking tour and cooking company. The media exposure was so strong that before long I was interviewed on radio, television, and in print about the experience. I took advantage of this golden opportunity to hone our company into what it is today: a dozen priceless tour leaders on staff, who well represent what our company offers on our unique walking tours. A typical day in my life is more of that old childhood combination of people and food. We meet hundreds of visitors each week who take our organized daily Wok Wiz Chinatown tours. I am in front of audiences to perform at cooking shows and classes, and write for numerous publications on food and travel.

Despite this hodgepodge of activities, my heart is never very far from where it all started, my parents' home in Chinatown. When I visit them, Mother meets me with a hug and the customary Chinese greeting "Have you eaten?" instead of "How are you?" If I have not eaten, she may be concerned. Perhaps I am not feeling well enough to eat? If I answer "yes," it opens the door for Mother to offer more food. There is always a pot of soup simmering on the stove, or chicken being cooked. Naturally, leftovers occupy space in the refrigerator—in case one of the Fong-Torres clan shows up hungry. I bring a bag full of fresh oranges or other fruits to add to an overflowing bowl set ceremoniously on the kitchen counter. Before we take our last nibble of Chinese sweet cake, or last spoonful of soup, Mother or Father asks, "Are you staying for dinner?" When my daughter Tina visits her grandparents, she is always asked what she wants for dinner, even though she is coming home in the afternoon! No matter what our financial situation was, our parents made certain that there was food on the table for their five children. Maybe that is why Dad got into the restaurant business to begin with, to be close to food so his family would not be far from it.

I welcome you into my kitchen, to use these recipes my mother taught me, or which were developed from skills learned from my restaurateur father, or created in cooking classes I've taught for the past 20 years. Some traditional recipes have been modified to incorporate new ideas in Chinese cooking. There are also recipes my colleagues have contributed and some creations from my newest culinary friends, the great chefs of Hawaii.

I hope every meal that you share with family and friends is a fun-filled and delicious dining experience. And I hope that these ideas sent from my kitchen to yours will help make those meals even more enjoyable.

方慧嫻

Shirley Fong-Torres

Before You Start:
A Note on Health and Ingredients

The recipes are clear-cut, and most are a snap to make. If some ingredients are not available in your home town, please try substitutions. I suggest some substitutes in the recipes, but there are undoubtedly many others waiting for the creative cook.

I have modified some of the recipes to incorporate new ideas in Chinese cooking. In line with today's interest in good health and nutrition, most of the recipes call for the minimum amount of cooking oil, the removal of chicken skin, and the use of fresh vegetables.

More people are serving brown rice instead of white because brown rice contains fiber, vitamins, and trace elements that are lost in the milling process. Try it and see if you like it.

Feel free to substitute brown sugar or honey for white sugar. Sugar is used sparingly in Chinese cooking, except for a dish such as Medallions of Pork in Sweet and Sour Sauce.

The relation between sodium and high blood pressure is common knowledge today. Therefore, I recommend the use of low-sodium products, such as low-sodium soy sauce. Look carefully at the labels. These recipes call for very little table salt. Because I use the minimal amount of it in cooking, there is not a recipe for a popular dish called Salt-Baked Chicken—I prefer to highlight marinades and quick stir-frying of fresh ingredients and seasonal vegetables.

As for monosodium glutamate, I never use it.

Finally, one of the more difficult aspects of completing this book was to indicate the number of servings for each recipe. This is not an easy task, because most Chinese meals are comprised of several courses, and how many one particular recipe serves will depend on the total number of diners, and their appetites.

Let's go wokking!

Chinese Kitchen Equipment

About Woks:

The first Chinese cooking tool I learned about was the wok, as most of my childhood was spent helping in my parents' restaurants. Dad's industry-size woks looked like hot tubs through my little girl eyes, but they held my fascination. Not surprisingly, I am in the cooking business today, and have many more woks than pots and pans in my kitchen. The wok is not only used for stir-frying, but for steaming, deep-frying, braising, even to make popcorn—keep the lid on!

The public's love for Chinese food and cooking keeps wok production companies busy, as they aim to meet the customers' demands and changing waves of cooking. Woks and stir-fry pans come in all sizes, designs, and materials. A 14-inch wok is one found in most home kitchens. A 12-inch wok is good as a supplementary wok, for cooking or deep-frying small amounts of food, and 9-inch woks are handy for making sauces and for single diners on a diet. It is difficult to say which is the best because there are so many excellent woks on the market today. The carbon steel woks were first introduced to the public by Bob Adamis, who founded Atlas Metal Spinning Co. in the 1920s in Chinatown, after being approached by Chinese restaurateurs. The Adamis family carries on the tradition with a successful wok manufacturing company in South San Francisco.

In addition to my dependable Atlas carbon steel wok, which I have had for over 15 years and still love to use, I have a whole new collection. My kitchen boasts woks made of stainless steel, cast iron, and with various non-stick components. For too many years to count, I have used Joyce Chen's Peking Pan until finally, the coating is beginning to show signs of age. Joyce Chen's Products, based in Massachusetts, introduced a new Chencote stir-fry pan that will probably last me another ten years. It is an improved version of the original model, has an excellent special non-stick coating, is fairly light in weight, and is easy to transport. Woks with coatings require less cooking oil and are easy to clean. Use wooden utensils to prevent scratching the delicate surfaces.

Le Creuset has a magnificent wok and stir fry pan that is made of cast iron. I like this wok's wide, deep rounded well, which makes it fun to stir-fry because it is easy to move food around its higher-than-standard sides. Le Creuset's wok and stir-fry pan are heavier than most others, but they are easy to work with, conduct heat beautifully, are very simple to clean, and do not rust. Although a cover is not included, simply use one that is in your kitchen—my 12 inch glass fry pan cover does a fine job.

Taylor and Ng is another highly respected wok manufacturing company. Established in the 1960s, the company has been successful from the beginning. Savvy marketing and a fun and trendy separate line of cooking-related products and accessories keep Taylor and Ng on the cutting edge in the industry. Other excellent woks and stir fry pans are made by reputable companies such as Meyer Corporation and Calphalon. I believe that every major kitchenware company has a wok to offer the consumer. Try different woks and frying pans to determine which is the best for you.

ELECTRIC WOK AND POT:

My Farbarware electric wok is almost 12 years old and still going strong. I like its deep well, and the heat conduction is even and goes up as high as necessary for stir-frying. It is absolutely one of my favorite electric woks. I use it primarily when I need a second wok, to deep-fry food, and for soups. An electric wok is perfect for entertaining, especially for Firepot Cooking for 4–5 people, and for soups. I use Zojirushi's Gourmet d'Expert electric pot to make Lions' Head Soup and for Firepot Cooking for two. It is handy to have a versatile electric wok or pot, as it frees a burner or two for cooking other dishes.

TO SEASON A WOK:

Before using a wok for the first time, clean and season it. Wash the wok thoroughly with hot soapy water to remove the oil applied during manufacturing. Dry it inside and out with paper towels, until the towel is clean. Place the wok on the stove over medium heat and pour a small amount of cooking oil on a clean paper towel. Rub the inside of the wok with the oiled towel to close the pores in the metal. Continue this procedure until the towel stays clean. After each use, wash the wok with a mild soap and a plastic scouring pad, and dry completely, rubbing a very small amount of oil in the well. A spun steel wok will darken after long use.

WOK UTENSILS:

The spatula (wok chann) and scooper (wok hauk) complete a wok set. They are approximately 12 inches long, made of stainless steel, bent to conform to the shape of a wok, and have small wooden handles. They are very handy to use when stir-frying, to mix food around, and to transfer food from wok to plate. Wooden utensils are suggested for any woks that have a coating, in order to prevent scratching the coated surface.

CLEAVER:

A sharp cleaver is an important tool in the kitchen. Use a cleaver to cut, slice, dice, mince, and crush. Use the wide blade to transfer food from the cutting board to the wok. Do not use a cleaver to hack up a chicken—use a meat chopper made specially for this purpose. A good cleaver fits your hand as comfortably as good shoes fit your feet. Select one that is comfortable and sharp. Serious cooks invest in an excellent cleaver, such as my friend Martin Yan's Chinese Knife. It is the only cleaver I use. It's very sharp and comfortable to hold. Wash the cleaver after every use with hot soapy water and dry it well. To insure its sharpness and longevity, keep it from contact with other cutting implements. Dull cleavers can be sharpened professionally, or with a high-quality electric sharpener such as one made by Chefs' Choice. The old-fashioned method is to use a sharpening steel or stone.

ELECTRIC RICE COOKERS:

An electric rice cooker is a welcome helper in the kitchen, especially during a dinner party. It gives the cook an extra burner since the rice cooks off the stove. There are several rice cookers on the market, ranging from small ones which cook up 2–3 cups of rice, perfect for singles and couples, to family-size cookers that hold 10 or more cups of rice. A good rice cooker has a temperature control that keeps the rice warm while the rest of the meal is being cooked. The Zojirushi Micom rice cooker is an exciting new product, worth the extra money if you value high-quality products and love to cook and entertain. It is a rice cooker with a brain, with settings for cooking regular long-grain rice, brown or sweet rice, and even for rice congee and soup. This remarkable rice cooker knows how much time is required to cook several types of rice properly. As with woks, shop around to see which rice cooker best fits your budget and needs.

CLAYPOTS:

Claypot cooking is very popular, and claypots are among the most ancient of cooking vessels. It is a fairly healthy method of cooking where marinated meat is often pan-fried or stir-fried, then stewed for a length of time. For the true health addict, skip the pre-frying and place marinated food directly into the claypot. A small amount of broth is added to the bottom of the cabbage or lettuce-lined claypot to prevent scorching or burning of the food, and to make a light sauce. Chinese claypots are also known as sand pots because the exterior is a coarse, sandy-textured beige, with a dark brown, smooth glazed interior. They come in various designs, with a single handle, a long handle covered with wire (to protect from breaking), and the larger ones take the shape of a modern casserole dish, with two small handles. They crack easily if not seasoned or cared for properly. Wash the inside and out with hot water, removing dust and residue before using. There should always be liquid in the pot to prevent it from cracking. Never place an empty claypot on heat. Because it is a fragile pot, take extra care when using and handling it. Chinese claypots are not used in the oven.

FIREPOT:

Firepot cooking is similar to the use of a fondue pot, except the foods in firepots are cooked in simmering broth, not fried in oil. It is a very healthful way to dine. A traditional firepot comes in the shape of a large funnel, attached to a tubular round that contains simmering broth. It is fueled by charcoal. It is more practical to use a large electric wok, although it does take away from the old-world charm. The old method is tedious, since you have to attend to the pot constantly. Broth is simmered in the firepot or electric wok. Basic seasonings such as ginger and green onions are scattered around. The party begins when previously sliced meat, poultry, and seafood are marinated and placed around the table, along with a variety of vegetables and seasonings. Everyone works at this party, cooking his or her own meal by choosing food, placing it in individual small nets, then cooking it in the broth for a minute or two. Have an assortment of dips and sauces available, and have fun!

YUNNAN POT:

A Yunnan pot is traditionally used to make herbal soups and for one particular steamed chicken dish. It is unique in appearance, resembling a casserole with a cover. The interior contains a little chimney in the center. Ingredients are scattered inside the pot around the chimney, covered, and placed inside a large steaming pot. Steam rises through the chimney, and the food is cooked by the continuous hot steam and mist. No added oil or fat are required, and the food cooks in its own juices. Chinese cooking and cooking products maven Joyce Chen introduced the Good Earth Steam Pot, of particular delight to the health-conscious diners.

STEAMERS:

Steaming is one of the most traditional and fuel-conserving methods of Chinese cooking. Some of the foods that we steam-cook are rice, whole or filets of fish, poultry, a variety of buns and dim sum dumplings, and for Chinese banquets, whole wintermelons filled with soup, minced meat, and seafood. Food that is steamed is generally simple: a fish with a dollop of black bean or other sauce, scattered with slivers of ginger and green onions; chicken that has been marinated, dim sum purchased in advance that is re-heated by steaming.

Tools for Steaming:

A WOK:

The easiest and most economical way to steam is to use any size wok and wok cover. Place a steamer rack that fits inside the wok that will keep the dish of food being steamed from touching the water on the bottom.

BAMBOO STEAMER:

Available in most Asian specialty shops and, as Chinese cooking grows in popularity, in many houseware departments of major stores, the bamboo steamer set is attractive and fun to use. Traditionally, it is sold by individual pieces, so put together a practical set by purchasing two tiers and a lid. For steaming, a wok is filled with enough water to almost touch the bottom tier. They generally come in 12-inch or 14-inch diameters, and for most homes, the 12-inch ones will fit perfectly in a 14-inch wok. In steaming food, the bubbling water in the bottom of the wok should not touch the dish of food that is being cooked. The food can be transferred from the wok to the table, so the bamboo steamer serves a dual purpose. I also use bamboo steamers at cooking shows to attractively showcase vegetables, or at home to hold fruits and vegetables. It is very handy and decorative.

To clean the bamboo steamer, use a stiff brush, hot water and soap. Dry completely before storing.

RACKS:

Several types of racks are available, made especially for steaming. The simplest way to create a homemade rack is to place a set of bamboo chopsticks criss-cross on the inside of the wok and balance the dish or pan of food to be cooked on the chopsticks. This might be a little tricky, however, so consider purchasing a rack—they are inexpensive. A flat, metal Chinese steaming tray is usually perforated and round and fits into the wok; a simple rack that looks like a tic-tac-toe grid is made of wood with inerlocking bars. The collapsible metal steamer baskets that are readily available in most department stores and hardware stores may also be used.

Chinese Cooking Techniques

STIR-FRYING:

Stir-frying is the quickest and most enjoyable way to cook Chinese food. It is a low-fat, low-calorie technique because it requires only small amounts of vegetable oil. Food is sliced or diced into small pieces, then tossed and stirred around in the wok over high heat. The higher the heat, the better it seals in the juices and flavors of the meat, poultry, and seafood during the cooking process. Stir-frying is similar to sautéing—food is cooked quickly, moved around the wok or pan constantly. Vegetables are usually stir-fried very quickly in just a little oil to retain nutrients, hold a good color, and have a crisp texture. Quick cooking means that vitamins are not boiled away. Stir-frying is a good method for anyone on a diet, or in a hurry. Health-conscious cooks who want to reduce use of oil even further should consider a wok with non-stick coating.

The following are quick steps for basic stir-frying:

1. Heat wok with small amount of oil, swirling to coat sides so food does not stick to one section of the wok

2. Toss in savories, usually ginger, garlic, or onion

3. Stir-fry pre-cut food over high heat for a few minutes

4. Add broth, a necessary step to make a sauce, and bring to a boil

5. Gradually stir in cornstarch mixture to bind the sauce

6. Drizzle with sesame or hot oil, and top with minced green onion or sprigs of Chinese parsley (cilantro).

STEAMING:

Steamed food is suggested for the diet-conscious over stir-frying, as steaming usually requires no additional oil, while it retains juices, nutrients, and natural good flavors. Steaming is a very traditional method of Chinese cooking, especially for fish and dim sum dumplings. To steam, water is simmered in a wok, a rack is placed in the wok, and the food is placed on a plate or bowl, which in turn rests on the rack. The rack keeps the plate of food above the boiling water level in the wok as it steam-cooks, always covered. All kinds of food can be steamed—fish, pork, chicken, eggs, even a dessert like steamed sponge cake.

Another way to steam is with bamboo steamers, which are usually sold in sets of two, with a matching cover. These steamers fit handily in the wok, and are great for making dim sum dishes, or for reheating food. They are very decorative as well, like hand-made baskets woven of natural material.

BLANCHING:

The only type of blanching I recommend is water blanching for hearty vegetables such as broccoli, cauliflower or long beans. This intensifies and brightens the color of the vegetables, which are added to the wok when meat and other vegetables are nearly cooked. The method used is simple: dip pieces of vegetable into boiling water for no more than 1 or 2 minutes and rinse in cold water. Some restaurant chefs oil-blanch meat, seafood, and vegetables, with the contention that this technique seals in juices and creates a sheen. I believe that if food is marinated correctly, the hot sizzle of a wok is enough to seal in flavors.

SIMMERING:

Simmering is a form of slow-cooking, assigned usually to soups, meat dishes, one-pot meals, and stews. Simmering creates flavors to integrate, and tenderizes tough meats. It is by far one of the simplest and most traditional of cooking techniques, not only in the Chinese kitchen. Heavy-duty pots or skillets with tight-fitting lids are usually used for simmering.

BRAISING:

Sometimes used as a step in claypot or slow cooking. Meat, poultry, or seafood is first browned in a wok over high heat to seal in marinade and natural juices. Then it is cooked in another wok or pot, over low heat with other ingredients and seasonings until the food is tender.

PAN-FRYING:

Very common in Chinese cooking, this method utilizes a shallow pan, and food is fried on one side, then turned over and fried on the other. Pan-fried noodles for chow mein cook beautifully in a 14-inch frying pan. I also like to use a non-stick frying pan to quick-cook prawns in their shells.

DEEP-FRYING:

Food is cooked in large amounts (2–3 cups) of hot oil, in a large pan or wok. If you're not cooking too much food, use a smaller wok, which requires less oil, and still is effective. Setting the temperature at 350 to 375 degrees is fairly accurate. Test the oil before frying by heating the oil and placing a wooden chopstick in the center of the wok. If the oil begins to bubble around the chopstick, the oil is ready. If you place food in the wok and it falls to the bottom, the oil is not ready; if it turns brown or black, it is too hot. For a clean finish to deep-fried food, strain the oil often to get rid of undesired crumbs that settle in the wok. Use a small strainer with a wooden handle or a handy rack that rests on one side of the wok where fried food is drained and excess oil goes back to the wok. These are easy to find in Chinese specialty stores, and are inexpensive.

ROASTING:

Famous Chinese entrées are Roast Duck and Roast Pork. Meat or poultry to be roasted is first rubbed down with soy sauce and seasoning, marinated for a length of time, then hung on a hook and slow-cooked over a wood-burning fire or roasting pit. This is not convenient or practical for most home kitchens, but the simplest way to roast at home is to line a baking pan with aluminum foil, place a rack over the foil, and place the meat on the rack or on hooks to cook. The aluminum foil makes clean-up easier.

SMOKING:

Tea-smoked duck, chicken, or fish is simple to achieve in the home kitchen, as the process is not nearly as complex as in years past. Today, smoking is a flavoring technique using a heavy-duty pot or wok, aluminum foil, a rack, tea leaves, and a fresh duck, chicken, or fish. Ingredients for smoking include a mixture of brown sugar, tea leaves, raw rice, and for added flavor, tangerine peel, peppercorn, and star anise. The smoking ingredients are burned in a tin-foil-lined pot or wok; meat or fish is placed on a rack, and the intense, complex smoke creates the rich flavors.

CLAYPOT COOKING:

This is one of my favorite methods of cooking because it is simple, and no additional oil is necessary. It brings us back to ancient roots, and is one of the healthiest ways to cook. A heavy clay or sand pot is used. Food is well-seasoned and/or marinated, added to the clay pot with a small amount of liquid to prevent the bottom from burning, and stewed over simmering heat until cooked.

RED COOKING:

Sugar, soy sauce, or hot chili paste and spicy sauces are some of the ingredients in red-cooked dishes. It is a form of stewing with large portions of meat and poultry, well marinated or seasoned, perhaps with pickled or salted ingredients. It is cooked over low heat after bringing the cooking liquid to a boil.

MICROWAVING:

Chinese cooking is technically so quick that a microwave is not necessary. However, a microwave oven can be a time-saver for some steps in cooking, such as soaking mushrooms (place in bowl with water to cover, microwave for 15 seconds on high or until water begins to boil); pre-cooking bean thread; reheating dim sum and other Chinese food; thawing frozen noodles or wrappers; and cooking vegetables or making quick meals like dried packaged noodle soups.

Chinese Ingredients

ANISE, STAR (BOK GOK):
Dried brown star-shaped pod with a seed in each of its 8 points forming a cluster. Imparts licorice flavor. An essential ingredient in Five Spice Powder. Used to flavor chicken, in stews and claypot dishes.

BABY CORN:
Pale yellow-colored young corn, commonly sold in 15-ounce cans. Little corn on the cobs which average 3–4 inches in length. Use in salads, soups, and stir-fry dishes. A colorful, crunchy addition to Chinese recipes.

BAMBOO SHOOTS:
Cone-shaped shoots of the bamboo plant, with color ranging from pale to bright yellow. To use, drain and rinse in cold water. Refrigerate unused portion in fresh water to cover. Fresh bamboo shoots, found in select stores in Chinatown and Chinese specialty shops, are best for cooking. Canned bamboo shoots are available in most food markets.

BASIL LEAVES, FRESH:
Basil is becoming popular in Asian cooking, and adds a refreshing bite to stir-fry dishes. Fresh Asian basil leaves are available in most Asian supermarkets.

BEAN CAKE, BEAN CURD, TOFU:
These terms are used interchangeably to describe the soybean extract that is a soft, cream-colored gel with a yogurt-like texture. Because it is low in calories, high in protein, and has no cholesterol, it is very popular with health-conscious diners. It is most commonly sold floating in water, or in four squares in a plastic container, but is also available deep-fried, pressed, or fermented. If possible, purchase fresh tofu in an Asian market. There are three textures of tofu: soft, usually for soups, because it is too delicate for stir-frying and will fall apart; medium-soft (Japanese variety) for soups or stir-frying, and firm, excellent for stir-frying and for stuffing. Tofu is quite bland, and relies on other strong-flavored ingredients and sauces for its appeal. It spoils easily, so check the expiration dates on packages. Keep tofu covered with water and refrigerated.

BEAN CURD SHEETS:

Used primarily in vegetarian cooking to simulate chicken and duck, for filling for vegetarian dim sum, such as Vegetarian Spring Rolls. Light brown sheets of dried bean curd are available in the frozen food section of large Asian supermarkets. They are usually wrapped in stacks of a dozen or more sheets, and must be handled delicately.

BEAN CURD STICKS:

Long, dried, brittle, and ivory-colored, bean curd sticks are sold in packages and are approximately 2 feet in length but folded in half. Must be soaked first, then used in soup or in traditional dishes such as Lo Han Jai (Buddhist Vegetarian Stew). Another dried variety of bean curd comes flattened in stiff thin sheets, and is used as a wrapper for vegetarian dim sum as well as for general cooking.

BEAN CURD, FERMENTED (FOO YEE):

An acquired taste for many, fermented bean curd is soaked in spices, wine, salt, and water. Available in bottles. Your first impression may be that it looks like cubes of old cheese. Very pungent, creamy, and earthy, it is used in steamed chicken or pork dishes, and is tasty when added to stir-fry garlic spinach or similar vegetable dishes.

BEAN CURD (TOFU), FRIED:

Just as the name indicates, these are cubes of deep-fried bean curd, approximately 1½ inches in size. When fried, a golden crust forms and the inside remains soft. Fried bean curd is sold by the pound, and is used in stir-fry and vegetarian dishes.

BEAN CURD (TOFU), PRESSED:

In this form, water is pressed out of bean curd when it is being made. Weight is placed on freshly-made curd to squeeze out excess liquid. The end product is a firm and drier bean curd. Unless plain pressed bean curd is desired, it is usually marinated in soy sauce, sugar, and star anise. In the market, pressed bean curd is sold in cellophane packages, and looks like cheese. It is available plain (white) or seasoned (dark brown). Pressed bean curd is an excellent substitute for meat in making dishes such as potstickers because it adds meatlike texture. To use, cut into thin slices or strips.

BEAN CURD, RED (NOM YEE):

A spicy bean curd similar to the fermented variety, used primarily to add flavor to steamed foods (e.g., spareribs, roast pork, duck) or as an accompaniment to other dishes.

BEAN SPROUTS:

From the mung bean, these snow-white sprouts with little yellow tops are best when purchased fresh. Do not choose them if they are limp or discoloring. Rinse in cold water and use as soon as possible—they do not hold well after a few days in the refrigerator and cannot be frozen. Approximate length: 2–3 inches.

BEAN THREADS, LONG RICE, (SAI FUN), CELLOPHANE NOODLES:

A semi-clear noodle also known as Chinese vermicelli. Made from mung bean starch, they are usually sold in 1-pound net bags, divided into 8 skeins of 2 ounces each, held together by pink or red bands. They expand after pre-soaking in warm water. Excellent stir-fried or in soups.

BIRDS' NESTS:

This food product comes from the saliva of a species of swallows. The twigs and feathers are washed away, and what remains is the saliva that glued the nest together. Considered a delicacy, the highest grade are the whole, but small cup-like pale brown nests. Birds' nests are rich in protein and vitamins, and are served as a soup at Chinese banquets and for very special dinners. I liked Birds' Nest Soup until I discovered its origin.

BITTERMELON:

Wrinkled green squash, 6–8 inches long. Also called a bitter gourd. True to its name, it is bitter, similar to a strong bell pepper. To prepare for cooking, cut bittermelon into halves; remove seeds, cut to bite-sized slices, and blanch 3–4 minutes before stir-frying to reduce the bitterness. Can also be cut into rings and stuffed with minced pork and shrimp prior to steaming. A definite acquired taste, especially if you have not grown up with it. Bittermelon is considered a health food because it contains quinine.

BLACK BEANS, FERMENTED:

Black soybeans which have been cooked and salted. They are sold in small cellophane packages. They are soft and sometimes seasoned with ginger. A highly popular soybean product used mostly in sauces (asparagus beef, prawns with lobster sauce, spareribs with black bean sauce), and for steaming with fresh fish. Black bean sauce is one of the most widely-used sauces in Cantonese cooking. Usually combined with minced garlic and soy sauce as a sauce, and with garlic and hot oil as a dip for dumplings.

BOK CHOY (CHOY SUM):

A fibrous Chinese cabbage, with white stems and large green leaves, looking somewhat like Swiss chard. Choy sum is the "heart" of the bok choy, smaller in appearance and generally more tender and tastier. Cooks rather quickly, excellent stir-fried or added to soup.

BROCCOLI, CHINESE (GAI LON):

A leafy vegetable with slender stalks, it retains an appealing green color when cooked properly, and is a little crunchy.

BROWN BEAN SAUCE, SOYBEAN PASTE (MIN SEE JEUNG):

Sometimes referred to simply as bean paste, this is a brown, salty, thick paste made of ground soybeans, flour, salt, and other ingredients. Used traditionally in recipes which include bean cake and minced ground pork. It completes a strong taste in Cantonese dishes such as a classic Bean Cake Chow Yuk, which would otherwise be quite bland. Available in jars and cans. Must be stored in refrigerator.

CELLOPHANE NOODLES:
See Bean threads.

CHILI PEPPER, CHILI OIL:
These products add a spicy heat to whatever is cooked. Chili peppers are used whole or minced in stir-frying. For the daring, chili oil is added to vegetable oil in the stir-frying stage. Be careful not to overuse this oil or chili peppers, as good food flavors may be masked by the power of the pepper or oil. One of my favorite commercial oils is House of Tsang's Mongolian Fire Oil. It will add a fiery sizzle to any stir-fry dish.

CHILI SAUCE OR PASTE:
A hot sauce or paste made with minced chili peppers, vinegar, and garlic. Ingredients vary by company, but it's always HOT! Available usually in jars. Use in cooking (Kung Pao Chicken, Garlic Chicken or Prawns), or as a condiment. One of my favorite brands is Lan Chi.

CHINESE PARSLEY:
See Cilantro.

CHINESE PEA PODS:
See Snow peas.

CHINESE SAUSAGE (LOB CHEUNG):
A very familiar ingredient in Chinese cooking. This reddish sausage is made of cured pork, lean pork, beef, or duck liver, and is usually sold in strings of two. The most commonly-used lob cheung is made with pork. Great in steamed foods, added to the rice pot, in soups, or minced and added to various fillings for dumplings. Keeps for weeks in the refrigerator or indefinitely in the freezer.

CHIVES, CHINESE (GOW CHOY):
Long and thin green leaves. From the onion family. These flat chives add a delicate onion flavor to food, and are excellent stir-fried with eggs, and added to dim sum dumplings. Sold by the bunch. Chives are quite fragile and last only a few days in the refrigerator.

CHIVES, YELLOW (GOW WONG):
Yellow chives taste similar to mild sweet onions, and are flatter than the Chinese chives described above. Grown with no exposure to sunlight, they remain yellow. They are sold by weight, and usually cost much more than other types of chives. The yellow color makes them very attractive in soup, stir-fry noodles, and dim sum dishes.

CILANTRO, CORIANDER, CHINESE PARSLEY:
Also known as Mexican parsley, depending on where you live. It has fragile green leaves and a strong, distinct flavor. Used for garnish or added to Chinese entrées, essential in Chinese Chicken Salad, Wintermelon Soup, and as a topping for Steamed Fish or Claypot Crab.

CLOUD EAR FUNGUS (WUN YEE, WOOD EARS, BLACK FUNGUS):

These little wrinkled-up hard-to-the-touch gems are an absolute must in preparing Mu Shu Pork, Hot and Sour Soup, and vegetarian dishes. Cloud ear fungus needs to be soaked in hot water before use. It can expand to at least triple the size. Wood ear is another fungus, larger than cloud ear fungus, and requires extra soaking time.

CORNSTARCH:

Essential in the Chinese pantry. Necessary in almost every stir-fry recipe which calls for a thickened sauce, and for marinating foods. A good binding agent for sauces and for making batter for deep-frying. A quick gravy mixture combines cornstarch with cold water. No Chinese chef is far from a container of cornstarch and water while cooking.

CURRY:

Curry powder and pastes come in varying degrees of flavors and heat. The best way to choose a curry powder or paste is to try different brands. Cooking enthusiasts make curry powder from scratch.

EGG ROLL OR SPRING ROLL WRAPPERS:

These thin sheets, approximately 6 inches square, are made from noodle dough. They are used for frying spring (egg) rolls. Available in most major supermarkets or Asian specialty food markets, in the frozen or refrigerated food departments.

EGGPLANT, ASIAN:

An attractive, slender eggplant, with a pale or deep purple skin. It is smaller, contains less pulp, and is more delicate than ordinary U.S. market eggplant. Excellent stir-fried with minced ground pork, garlic and chili paste.

EGGS, SALTED DUCK:

Duck eggs are preserved in salt water for months. As the yolk hardens, it becomes a bright orange. Used by some Chinese chefs in steaming minced meat and ginger, or for mooncakes. If you think this is a little unusual, read on.

EGGS, THOUSAND-YEAR-OLD:

Duck eggs are just preserved for a few months—not a thousand years—in lime, salt, and ashes. The egg white becomes gelatinous and brownish black, and the egg yolk becomes blue-black. Adds earthy flavor to rice congee, or served on its own, cut into slices alongside preserved ginger.

FISH SAUCE (NAM PLA):

In Thailand, fish sauce is traditionally used in Southeast Asian cooking, but is appearing in Chinese pantries as well. Made of fermented and salted fish, it is clear and salty. Anchovy aficionados will take to this sauce with gusto.

FISH, SALTED (HOM YEE):

Preserved whole fish of many varieties from tiny sardine-types to king fish and flounder. Steamed with ginger and drizzled with minced green onions and hot oil, it is good served over rice. Also cooked into fried rice. A popular dish to order in restaurants is Chicken with Salt Fish Fried Rice.

FIVE-SPICE POWDER:

A powdered blend of fennel, Szechuan peppercorns, star anise, cinnamon, and cloves. Available in most food markets. Used to marinate roasted pork and chicken, in stewed dishes, and in some salads.

FUNGUS, BLACK:

See Cloud ear fungus.

FUZZY SQUASH, HAIRY SQUASH (MO GWA):

Oval-shaped green squash with a fuzzy surface. Remove fuzz with butter knife. Maintains a firm texture while taking on added flavors well. Subtle taste on its own. Looks like a tiny wintermelon with a fuzzy surface. May be stir-fried or used in soup recipes. Especially good combined with black mushrooms and tofu.

GARLIC:

Garlic is used for flavoring oil, for stir-frying, minced for marinating, and is a staple in Chinese cooking. Garlic is easy to crush by smacking with the side of a Chinese cleaver and popping the clove from its peel before mincing.

GINGER ROOT:

Fresh ginger root is a must for most Chinese dishes. It can be minced, sliced, chopped, grated, and used in marinating or general cooking. Ginger is a rhizome which resembles knuckles of a hand. Has a distinct, spicy flavor. Available in most supermarkets today, and plentiful in any Asian market. Irregular shapes of these knobby roots come in all sizes. Can be peeled and placed in a jar of sherry to cover, and refrigerated. If used frequently, may be left out in a dry area, and cut off as much as you need. Freezing reduces flavor over long term. Young ginger has lobes with pinkish points, must be used as soon as possible, and has a delicate, light flavor, preferred as an accent in soup.

GINKGO NUTS:

Small white nuts with hard shells and small, yellow-ivory-colored meat. Considered an excellent source for cleansing one's system, and for good luck. Comes from a tree native to China. Must be shelled and blanched before cooking. Good in soups, a must in Lo Han Jai, the traditional Buddhist Vegetarian Stew served during Chinese New Year, and good in slow-cooking stews. Ginkgo nuts are not used uncooked.

GINSENG ROOT:

Ginseng root comes in various shapes, and is dried and pale brown. The root helps to regulate blood pressure, and helps the body cope with stress. It is very popular, used in tea, in cooking, and in medicine. Ginseng root grows in the floor of hardwood forests; it needs a great deal of shade and excellent drainage. Ginseng from Korea is considered the best. However, large quantities of ginseng are grown in China and the United States, especially in the great state of Wisconsin.

GOLDEN NEEDLES:

See Lily buds.

HOISIN SAUCE:

A reddish-brown, sweet and pungent sauce made from soybeans, spices, vinegar and chili, and depending on the brand, other ingredients as well. Excellent as a marinade for roast pork or spareribs. I prefer the Koon Chun brand, sold in Chinatown and in many supermarkets.

LEMON GRASS:

Lemon grass is available by the stalk. It is easy to identify in Asian food markets: up to 2 feet in length, pale yellow-green, and fibrous. Adds a nice lemony flavor to soups and stir-fry dishes. Only the lower part is used—crush the bulblike base to impart more flavor from this fragrant grass. An idea: cut the tough outer leaves into 3–4 inch pieces, and stick them between the skin and meat of a chicken before roasting.

LILY BUDS, LILY STEMS, GOLDEN NEEDLES, TIGER LILY BUDS:

Dried golden-colored lily buds averaging 3–4 inches long, usually sold in cellophane bags. Must be soaked before use. A necessity in recipes for Mu Shu Pork, Hot and Sour Soup, vegetarian dishes, and steamed with pork or poultry. Usually paired with cloud ear fungus.

LONG BEANS, CHINESE (DOW GAWK):

Also called mile-long beans, they are at least 18 inches in length. They resemble green beans, but are milder in taste. There are two varieties, a pale and a dark green. Both are wondrous, stir-fried with meat, poultry, or shellfish, and fermented black beans.

LONG RICE:

See Bean threads.

LOTUS LEAVES:

Lovely dried leaves of water-lily plants, they are usually round-shaped and about 12–14 inches in diameter. Lotus leaves, roots, and seeds are used in Chinese cooking and as medicine. The leaves are used to wrap sticky rice and chicken, pork, and mushrooms in a popular steamed dim sum dish. Lotus leaves impart an aromatic flavor to steamed food. Occasionally fresh lotus leaves are available in Chinese food markets.

LOTUS ROOT, WATER LILY ROOT:

Pale brown stem of the water lily. Looks like potatoes that are attached to each other. Varies in size. When cut across the grain, the root has an attractive snowflake design. Used in stuffed taro dim sum, and in soups and stews. Texture is similar to a potato, but it is tastier. Also used sweetened and carmelized as a candy. Lotus root is grown throughout China.

LOTUS SEEDS:

Small lotus seeds are traditionally served at Chinese festive occasions, candied or used in desserts. Available in small plastic bags, they are believed to help combat insomnia.

MAI FUN:
See Rice sticks.

MIN SEE JEUNG:
See Brown bean sauce.

MIN SEE SAUCE:
See Soybean paste.

MONOSODIUM GLUTAMATE, MSG:
Stay away from these tiny white crystals considered to be a flavor enhancer. MSG is not necessary if food is fresh and properly prepared. Some people are highly allergic to MSG and eating food containing it can cause headaches and hives. I recommend that you request your food without MSG at all restaurants. If you are allergic to MSG, it is important to carefully read the ingredients label on prepared Chinese food products (e.g., some oyster sauces contain MSG).

MUSHROOM, CHINESE BLACK, SHIITAKE (DOONG GOO):
A very popular item in Chinese cooking, mushrooms are sold dried, usually in cellophane packages. Comes in many grades. High quality dried mushrooms are thick and have cracks on them. Must be soaked in hot water and re-hydrated before cooking.

MUSHROOM, GRASS OR STRAW:
These mushrooms are readily available in cans, and are a good substitute for fresh or dried mushrooms. Must be rinsed prior to use; good in stir-fry dishes and in stews.

NOODLES:
Many varieties of noodles are available in Chinese food markets and noodle factories. There are fresh noodles, dried rice, egg, and wheat noodles in packages, and an assortment of noodles with various names depending on origin. Wheat noodles are available fresh and dried, known as "mein" in Chinese. Long and thin, these noodles are the most popular throughout Asia and in the United States as well. Egg noodles are made from a dough of wheat flour and eggs, and are very popular for chow mein dishes. Japanese noodles are made from buckwheat flour (soba noodles) or thick wheat noodles (udon). Rice noodles are available fresh, and are simple to cook. Just cut to bite-sized pieces, and stir-fry according to recipe. Fresh rice noodles are made from ground rice with water added to form a rice milk, which is then steamed into sheets of noodles. Dried rice noodles are soaked, drained, and used for cooking. Rice sticks come in cellophane bags, and are not boiled. They are deep-fried in small batches, traditionally used in Chinese Chicken Salad and as an attractive base for many stir-fry dishes. Starch noodles are always chewy. The most well-known starch noodles are bean threads, also called cellophane noodles. These thin noodles must be soaked or boiled in hot water first, then drained, rinsed in cold water, and stir-fried. Excellent in claypot recipes.

OIL, CHILI PEPPER:
See Chili pepper, Chili oil.

OIL, CHINESE SESAME:

A highly-refined fragrant oil obtained from the sesame seed. No comparison to the sesame oil found in most health food stores. It is wonderful in soups and some stir-fried dishes as a seasoning oil, but is not used as a cooking oil. Sesame oil has a strong, rich flavor, and is concentrated, so use sparingly. Stored in a cool place, this oil will last indefinitely.

OIL, PEANUT OR VEGETABLE:

Both are recommended for Chinese cooking because they withstand high heat and can rise to a high temperature without burning, and do not have an off smell or aftertaste. Olive oil is excellent for Italian cooking, but is too heavy for Chinese food. Flavored oils are also gaining popularity with the home cook as they can save some preparation time. Try a few brands to see which works best for you. I favor House of Tsang's Wok Oil because it is very aromatic with natural flavors of garlic and ginger. Tung Fong and Planters peanut oils are highly recommended.

OKRA, ASIAN (SING GWA):

A light green, long and narrow vegetable that resembles a cucumber, with hard, tough ridges that must be peeled before cooking. Cut in triangular pieces for soups, or diagonally in thin pieces for stir-frying. Can also be cubed into small pieces and added at the last minute to soups.

ONG CHOI:

See Water spinach.

ONION:

A variety of onions are used in Chinese cooking: yellow and white onions, green onions, chives, Chinese chives (at least a foot long, dark green leaves), yellow chives (sweet, delicate onion flavor with thin, pale yellow leaves). For variety, use a combination of several onions. Onion adds a special flavor to anything you cook.

OYSTER, DRIED (HO SEE):

Brown, hard-to-the-touch dried oysters with a heady taste. Used primarily in stewed food, such as Lo Han Jai, and simmered in soup, steamed or stir-fried. Must be soaked prior to use.

OYSTER SAUCE (HO YOW):

Made from essence of oysters, this sauce imparts an exotic and unique flavor. It does not have a very strong fishy taste, and is used in beef and vegetable dishes, and some soups (Won Ton with Oyster Beef). There are many varieties and grades of oyster sauce in the market. Read the label and purchase one that does not contain monosodium glutamate (MSG).

PEPPER, BLACK AND WHITE:

Both are used in Chinese cooking, each with a distinctive flavor. I prefer using white pepper in cooking for its lighter appearance and flavor. If possible, use fresh peppercorns as opposed to the pre-ground.

PICKLED VEGETABLES, CHINESE:

A variety of vegetables such as turnip, ginger, carrot, and cucumbers, shredded thinly and pickled. Sold in jars, cans, or homemade. Used in noodle dishes, added at the last minute to some stir-fried beef and chicken dishes, or as a topping for Chinese rice congee.

PLUM SAUCE:

A golden-colored fairly thick sauce with bits of plum, flavored with chili, sugar, and vinegar. The sauce is lightly spicy, yet sweet and pungent. It is used as a condiment for roast duck and deep-fried appetizers such as fried prawns and spring (egg) rolls. Sold in bottles and jars, it must be refrigerated.

POMELO:

A yellow fruit that resembles an oversized grapefruit. Pomelos are very popular around Chinese New Year for displays along with platters of oranges and tangerines. The pomelo's bright yellow color and massive size represent great prosperity.

RED DATES (HOONG DAW):

Small, dried, wrinkled up deep-red fruit used in medicinal soups as well as for slow-cooked and stewed, home-style dishes. Must be soaked prior to use. Red dates add a gentle sweetness to Bean Curd Stick Soup.

RICE FLOUR:

A flour milled from long-grain rice, usually sold in 1-pound packages. Used primarily for pastries and dumplings.

RICE STICKS:

Skinny translucent dried noodles resemble sai fun (cellophane noodles). Mai fun is made from rice flour, and is traditionally deep-fried and used in Chinese Chicken Salad or as a base garnish for stir-fried dishes.

RICE WINE:

One of the most widely-used is Shao-Hsing wine, for marinating food as well as for social drinking. If Chinese rice wine is not available in your home town, substitute a good quality dry sherry.

RICE:

Long-grain rice (Texas and California are popular) is traditionally served with Chinese food. Jasmine rice is aromatic and lighter in texture. Sweet rice is a short-grain rice that is also called sticky, or glutinous rice. Glutinous rice is short-grain and sticky, used in stuffings or dim sum desserts. Basmati rice originates in India and is gaining popularity in Chinese cooking, along with brown rice for health-conscious diners.

SALT:

I use as little table salt in my recipes as possible. There is sodium in the soy sauces and other sauces. If you leave out salt, you may discover a whole world of intriguing food flavors that were masked by the salt. In some recipes, however, salt draws out flavors.

SALTED BLACK BEANS:
See Black beans, fermented.

SALTED OR DRIED FISH:
See Fish, salted.

SAUSAGE, CHINESE:
See Lob cheung.

SEAWEED HAIR, DRIED (FOT CHOY):
Resembles a pile of matted black hair. Does not look or sound appealing, but this variety of seaweed is nutritious and is traditionally used in Chinese Vegetarian Stew during Chinese New Year, as well as in casseroles. In Chinese, "fot choy" has the same sounds as the word "prosperity," so this ingredient is revered for festive occasions.

SEAWEED, DRIED (GEE CHOY):
Called "gee choy," which means paper vegetables, this seaweed indeed resembles thin sheets of purple paper. Highly nutritious, dried seaweed must first be soaked, then is used in soup. Has a subliminal fishy taste.

SESAME OIL:
See Oil, Chinese sesame.

SHARK'S FIN:
A seafood delicacy beloved by the Chinese people. It is very expensive, sold dried, and appears transparent with a pale gold coloring. It is the cartilage of the shark's fin, dried and used throughout the world in Asian restaurants and family kitchens for soup and dim sum dumplings. It has a subtle fish flavor, and when cooked, the cartilages separate into golden noodle-like threads. A must for Chinese wedding banquets and important festive occasions.

SHRIMP SAUCE, SHRIMP PASTE (HOM HAH):
A salty, strong and pungent shrimp paste. Contained in jars, gray color, reminiscent of anchovy paste. Popular in country-style Chinese cooking, steamed with pork or chicken.

SHRIMP, DRIED:
Very tiny, less than one inch long, these shrimp are found in cellophane bags, or loose in bins to pick and choose. They are used to season various foods, cooked with rice or rice noodles. They taste quite salty, and need to be soaked in water before using.

SNOW PEAS:
Also called Chinese pea pods, or sweet peas. They are green, flat pods and taste crunchy unless overcooked. Snow peas are easy to grow in your garden. When shopping, look for pods that are not longer than 2 ½ inches, have no marks and are firm to the touch, not limp. The end must be snipped first and strings removed if necessary. Home-grown snow peas often do not need to be strung. They are delicious freshly picked. Used the world over in Chinese cooking and salads.

SNOW PEA LEAVES:

Fairly new on the food scene, these lovely and tender leaves are from the snow pea plant. Gathered, trimmed, and rinsed, they are spectacular stir-fried quickly to a shimmering green with a little garlic and broth.

SOYBEAN PASTE:

See Brown bean paste.

SOY SAUCE:

Made from fermented and processed soybeans, with salt added. Soy sauce is an essential and indispensable ingredient in Chinese cooking. Black soy is used most frequently for cooking. It has good flavor and a dark color. Thin or light soy is lighter in appearance, and is used as a dip or in stir-frying where little color is desired. Thin or light soy differs from low-sodium or less-salt soy. Try a few different brands to find the one you like best. I recommend Koon Chun and Kikkoman black soy sauces, and especially the latter's low-sodium and less salt varieties.

SPRING ROLL WRAPPERS:

See Egg roll wrappers.

SWAMP CABBAGE:

See Water spinach.

TANGERINE PEEL, DRIED (GAW PAY):

Upon meeting an uncle in Hong Kong for the first time, I opened what I thought was a gift box of cookies, and it was filled with dried tangerine peel. Little did I know then what a healthful and special gift it was. Also sold as dried orange or mandarin orange peel, the older they are, the better the quality is considered to be. It is a favorite flavor addition to duck, and used with meats, especially in simmering, claypot dishes, in soups, and rice congee. Tangerine peel can be very expensive, especially if it has aged for decades. Rehydrate for 10–15 minutes before cooking, save soaking water to use in flavoring food and gravy.

TARO (WOO TAO):

Resembles a potato, available in varying sizes. Taro has a dark brown rough texture and tiny purple specks. Fancy Asian restaurants make fried baskets out of shredded taro, filled with combination seafood and vegetables. In teahouses, look for puffed up "Stuffed Taro Balls." Taro can also be steamed into a cake, stir-fried or cooked in stewed dishes, or sliced thin and deep-fried for a snack, taro chips. In Hawaii, taro is used for an island specialty, poi.

TIGER LILY BUDS:

See Lily buds.

TOFU:

See Bean cake, Bean curd.

TOFU, FRIED:

See Bean curd, fried.

TURNIP (LO BOK):

Resembles a large, white horseradish or daikon. Delicate in flavor, used diced up in stews, stir-fried dishes, or soup. Available almost year-round.

WATER SPINACH, SWAMP CABBAGE (ONG CHOY):

Very popular vegetable that is also referred to as Swamp Spinach. Water spinach comes in enormous bunches, with long stems and slender green leaves. Prepared like spinach, especially good quickly stir-fried with garlic or fermented bean curd.

WATERCHESTNUTS, CHINESE:

Fresh waterchestnuts taste like sweet jicama or coconut, and are small with a dark brownish-black covering which must be peeled before use. This sweet root vegetable is the bulb of a water grass grown in the flooded rice paddies of China. Waterchestnuts are available in most Asian specialty stores. It is easier to find canned waterchestnuts in food markets, but there is no comparison with the fresh ones, which are crisp and sweet. Choose fresh waterchestnuts which are hard as a rock, not wrinkled up with soft spots. Peel the waterchestnuts, place them in a bowl with cold water to cover until ready for cooking. Use for stir-frying and for snacks.

WHEAT STARCH:

A white powder that is used as an alternative to cornstarch as a thickener, and used to make the delicate, white, see-through wrapper for popular dim sum dishes, one of which is Steamed Shrimp Dumpling.

WINTERMELON:

Looks like a large watermelon. It is actually a large vegetable with a green skin and white and pulpy flesh. Wintermelons are sold in sections or whole in Asian supermarkets, and can weigh as much as 20 pounds. Wintermelon does not have much flavor, and is used primarily in soups. For special dinners, steam the whole wintermelon. Cut the top part off, remove the pulp and seeds, fill the cavity with chicken broth and other ingredients, and steam the wintermelon. Serve the soup right out of the self-made wintermelon soup tureen. Wintermelon has a cooling effect on the body.

WON TON WRAPPERS:

Thin, approximately 3-inch squares of noodle dough made from flour and eggs, used for fried or steamed Asian dim sum dumplings and won tons. Available in most supermarkets and Asian specialty food shops, usually in the refrigerated or frozen food departments.

WOOD EARS:

See Cloud ear fungus.

Appetizers and Savories

Asian Chicken Wings

Chinese-Style Roast Pork—Cha Sil

Connie's Taro Cakes

Crab or Smoked Salmon Puffs

Dad's Special Sweet Spring Rolls

Festive Sweet Turnovers

Firecracker Prawns

Fried Tofu with Dipping Sauce

Hoisin Sauce Chicken Wings

Lollipop Drumsticks

Lotus Leaf Chicken

My Father's Chinese Deep-Fried Egg Puffs—Jah Donn

Popular Spring Rolls

Potstickers

Seafood Spring Rolls

Simple Shrimp Toast

Steamed Pork Buns (Cha Sil Bow)

Tina's Onion Pancakes

Tofu Fried Won Ton with Sweet and Sour Sauce

Many popular appetizers and treats are included in this section. Some of them, like the Spring Rolls, Chinese New Year Turnovers, and the Steamed Pork Bow (the longest recipe in this book) are traditional. Others presented here are those my friends and relatives have created. My father, mother, father-in-law, and daughter all have a hand in this section.

Nibbling on a variety of these as appetizers is an excellent prelude to the main dinner event. They are also tasty party snacks and good contributions to potlucks.

A number of these treats are sold almost everywhere: pastry shops, restaurants or by sidewalk vendors. But many people like to try making them from scratch, and my cooking students often ask me to share my recipes for these treats.

Some of the recipes may appear rather complicated for apparently simple snacks, and you might even feel intimidated by some of the long lists of ingredients. Don't panic. These recipes are easier than they appear at first glance. If you prepare ingredients in advance and have them well organized, the final composition will be surprisingly easy. It can also be fun to "mass produce" these savories by having a few friends help you put them together.

Enjoy these treats with combinations of the sauces and dips made from recipes in the Basic Sauces and Dips section of this book.

Asian Chicken Wings

This is my father-in-law Bernard Carver's contribution. My family looks forward to everything he cooks, but this is one of our favorites. We jazzed it up with some Asian spices and seasonings. Adjust the amount of cayenne pepper and chili peppers according to taste.

10 chicken wings
1 cup all-purpose flour
1 teaspoon five-spice powder
½ teaspoon cayenne pepper

SAUCE
2 teaspoons vegetable oil
6 small chili peppers, crushed
  (optional)
¼ cup chicken broth
1 tablespoon soy sauce
¼ teaspoon hot-chili
  sesame oil
cayenne pepper to taste
Chinese parsley (cilantro)

Cut chicken wings into 3 pieces. Discard tips or reserve for chicken stock. Rinse chicken and towel dry. In a plastic bag, place flour, five-spice powder, and cayenne pepper. Add chicken and shake to coat all the wings.

Line baking pan with aluminium foil for easy clean-up. Coat rack in baking pan with oil or non-stick spray. Heat oven to 425 degrees. Place chicken wings on rack in baking pan and cook wings for 45 minutes or until done, turning once. During the last few minutes of cooking, heat a wok with vegetable oil, and add chili peppers. When they begin to turn black, remove and discard. Lower heat, add chicken broth, soy sauce, hot-chili sesame oil, and cayenne pepper to taste. When the chicken wings are golden brown, remove from oven and transfer to toss quicky in wok with sauce, just enough to lightly coat the chicken. Serve on a bed of Chinese parsley.

Makes 10 wings and drumettes.

Chinese–Style Roast Pork (Cha Sil)

In Chinatowns throughout the United States and in Asia, various types of cooked meat are on display, hanging on hooks and skewers. Chinese-style roast pork, whole roast duck and chicken are common sights to behold through the front windows of restaurants and food shops. This is a traditional and classic way to cook pork. Excellent with hot mustard dip.

Marinate the pork overnight for best results. This recipe can be prepared as a hot or cold appetizer, or to be added to many recipes such as fried rice, or used as a filling for spring rolls and steamed pork buns. It also freezes well.

---

2 pounds boneless pork butt

MARINADE
½ cup hoisin sauce
½ cup tomato catsup
¼ cup rice wine or dry sherry
¼ cup soy sauce
1 teaspoon sesame oil
3 cloves garlic, minced
1 teaspoon green onion,
   minced
¼ cup brown sugar
1 tablespoon honey

Trim excess fat from pork and cut into strips approximately 8-by-2-by-2 inches. Combine marinade ingredients in a large bowl and mix with strips of pork. Cover and marinate in refrigerator for at least 2 hours or overnight, turning occasionally.

Heat oven to 350 degrees. Remove pork from bowl of marinade. Reserve remaining marinade for basting. Place pork on the rack of baking pan lined with aluminum foil. Add ½ cup water to bottom of pan. Bake the pork for 30 minutes, basting occasionally with reserve marinade. Turn and baste the other side, and bake for an additional 15–20 minutes. Switch the oven to broil setting and broil meat on each side for 2 minutes to give it a glazed coating. Cool for 15 minutes before cutting into thin pieces to serve.

Serves 6–8.

Connie's Taro Cakes (Woo Tao Go)

This is a traditional dim sum (Chinese teahouse) favorite, served as a snack, or part of a luncheon party. I usually do not like taro, but my mother has a way of preparing it so that it is firm and delicious. My daughter Tina visited Grandma one day and got this secret recipe.

1 tablespoon vegetable oil
4 cloves garlic, minced
1 cube of preserved bean curd (red nom yee) (optional)
1 pound taro, peeled, rinsed, cut into ½-inch cubes
3 tablespoons dried shrimp, soaked for 10 minutes
½ cup minced Chinese-style roast pork
2 links of Chinese sausage (lob cheung)
2 green onions, minced
1 teaspoon salt
1 teaspoon cornstarch
1 teaspoon soy sauce
1 teaspoon sesame oil
1 pound rice flour

Heat wok with 2 teaspoons oil, swirling to coat sides. Stir-fry the garlic, bean curd, and taro, and add enough water to cover. Cover and simmer until taro is soft, approximately 15 minutes.

In another frying pan, add remaining oil and stir-fry shrimp, Chinese-style roast pork, Chinese sausage, and green onion, and add ¼ teaspoon salt, cornstarch, soy sauce, and sesame oil. Stir for 1 minute and remove to a bowl.

In another large bowl, mix rice flour with 3 cups water and ¾ teaspoon salt and mix well. Add the cooked taro and mix well. Place a 10-inch pie pan on rack in a wok prepared for steaming, with water added. Pour taro mixture into pan. Stir in half of the shrimp and meat mixture. Cover, turn heat down to simmer, and steam for 45 minutes. Sprinkle remaining shrimp and meat over top and steam another 15 minutes. Cool completely before cutting into diamond shapes or wedges.

Yields 1 round taro cake, 10 inches in diameter.

Crab or Smoked Salmon Puffs

The first time I attempted to make these puffs, I tried to duplicate the Crab Rangoon that my father introduced to me at Trader Vic's restaurant, where he was a chef. Since I didn't have a recipe, I made the mistake of using too much cream cheese. This is an improved version. They are delicious dipped with Sweet and Sour Plum Sauce, and suggested as an appetizer.

½ pound cooked crab meat or smoked salmon, lightly flaked
1 teaspoon green onion, finely-minced
¼ pound cream cheese (at room temperature)
½ teaspoon steak sauce
¼ teaspoon garlic powder or 2 cloves minced garlic
1 pound won ton wrappers
1 beaten egg or 2 egg whites
3 cups vegetable oil

Combine crab meat or smoked salmon, green onion, cream cheese, steak sauce, and garlic. Place ½ teaspoon of mixture in center of won ton wrapper; fold square over to form a triangle. Lightly brush the center with the beaten egg. Bring opposite corners together and press gently, so filling will be secure. Place oil in wok and heat to 375 degrees for deep-frying. Deep-fry one crab or salmon puff and adjust heat downwards if necessary. Fry rest of puffs until delicately brown, less than 2 minutes. Serve hot.

Makes 40–50.

Dad's Special Sweet Rice Spring Rolls

When I first introduced these spring rolls to my cooking class in 1975, the students were surprised with this delicious twist to a traditional and classic favorite. Hot mustard and soy sauce are suggested for dipping.

FILLING
1 lean Chinese sausage (lob cheung)
1 chicken breast, cooked, skinned, boned, and minced

Cook Chinese sausage in hot water for 3–4 minutes and mince into small pieces.

Heat wok. Add teaspoon vegetable oil. Stir-fry chicken, ham, Chinese sausage, and green onion for 1 minute. Add soy

4 ounces cooked ham,
  minced
2 tablespoons green
  onion, minced
2 tablespoons soy sauce
¾ cup cooked glutinous rice
1 teaspoon sesame oil

OTHER INGREDIENTS
1 pound spring roll wrappers
3 cups vegetable oil
1 egg, beaten (to seal rolls)

sauce and continue to cook another 2–3 minutes. Stir in the pre-cooked glutinous rice, and blend all the ingredients. Add the sesame oil. Remove filling from wok and cool for at least 30 minutes.

To assemble spring rolls, place a heaping tablespoon of the filling in the center of a wrapper. Bring bottom of wrapper towards the top corner, and bring sides together. Roll, and seal with a little egg splash. Heat a wok with 3 cups vegetable oil. Deep-fry the spring rolls for approximately 3–4 minutes, until golden brown. Remove and drain well. Cool for 15 minutes. Cut into halves or thirds.

Makes 10.

Festive Sweet Turnovers

Sweet turnovers are traditionally served at Chinese New Year get-togethers to start the year with something sweet tasting. Serve as a snack, and make an extra batch for Chinese New Year.

1 pound won ton skins

FILLING
½ cup shredded coconut
¾ cup roasted peanuts, finely
  chopped
¼ cup white sugar
¼ cup brown sugar
1 tablespoon toasted sesame
  seeds
1 egg, beaten

OTHER INGREDIENTS
3 cups vegetable oil for deep-
  frying

To prepare the filling, place the coconut, peanuts, white and brown sugar and toasted sesame seeds in a medium-sized bowl and mix well. Scoop a teaspoon of filling in the center of individual won ton skins. Fold each skin into a triangle. Use beaten egg to seal edges. Fill a wok with oil. Deep-fry turnovers, a few at a time, until golden brown (this usually takes less than 1 minute). May be sprinkled with sugar before serving.

Makes approximately 40.

Firecracker Prawns

These are excellent for appetizers or the first course of a meal. The combination of oil, salt, and prawns cooked over high heat adds to this tasty and aromatic dish. We Chinese are used to eating the crunchy prawn shells too, but be very careful eating the shells if you haven't attempted this before.

1 pound fresh large or tiger prawns, rinsed and unshelled
3–4 slices fresh ginger, approximately 1 by 2 inches
2 green onions, white part mashed, green part cut into 1-inch pieces
1 tablespoon soy sauce
2 tablespoons rice wine or dry sherry
2 teaspoons chicken broth
3 tablespoons vegetable oil
½ teaspoon salt
⅛ teaspoon hot chili pepper oil

With a small knife, gently cut the back of each prawn, through the shell, about ¼ inch to reveal and remove the black intestinal vein. Cut ½ of the ginger into matchstick-sized pieces and mince the rest. Cut the green onion into 1-inch slanted pieces. Combine soy sauce, wine, and chicken broth.

Heat wok with oil, swirling to coat sides. When the oil begins to smoke, quickly toss in prawns, ginger, and green onion. Stir-fry constantly for 1–2 minutes. When prawns begin to turn pink, sprinkle in salt and chili pepper oil. Gradually, add the soy sauce, wine, and chicken broth mixture. Continue to stir-fry another 2–3 minutes, until liquid reduces completely.

Fried Tofu with Dipping Sauce

This is simple, delicious, and fairly healthy. Thanks to my good friend, Chinese cooking expert Rhoda Wing, for this simple recipe. The deep-fried tofu is also delicious added to any vegetables, seafood, meat or poultry.

4 cakes fresh, firm tofu, approximately 3-inch cubes
3 cups vegetable oil

Drain tofu on paper towel for an hour. Cut into 1-inch cubes. Heat a wok with 3 cups oil to 375 degrees. Place 1 cube of

DIPPING SAUCE
1 teaspoon chili oil
2 teaspoons vegetable oil
2 teaspoons soy sauce
1 teaspoon sugar
1 tablespoon sesame paste
  or creamy peanut butter

tofu in to test heat, adjusting if necessary. Deep-fry the tofu a few cubes at a time until golden brown. Drain well with paper towels. Place dipping sauce ingredients in a small bowl and mix into a smooth paste. Serve with fried tofu.

Hoisin Sauce Chicken Wings

This is good served hot or cold, and recommended for potluck, parties, or picnics. If excess sauce remains after cooking, advance heat, stir continuously until sauce reduces.

20 chicken wings

MARINADE FOR CHICKEN
2 tablespoons hoisin sauce
1 tablespoon soy sauce
1 teaspoon minced garlic
4 tablespoons rice wine or
  dry sherry
1 teaspoon cornstarch

OTHER INGREDIENTS
1 tablespoon vegetable oil
½ cup chicken broth
2 green onions cut into 1½-
  inch slivers lengthwise

Separate wing from little drumsticks. Rinse and pat dry. Combine the hoisin sauce, soy sauce, garlic, wine, and cornstarch in a large bowl. Add the chicken wings and marinate for 30 minutes or longer. Drain excess marinade, if any remains in the bowl, and reserve to add to wok while cooking.

Heat wok with oil, swirling to coat sides. When the oil is smoky, stir in the chicken and stir-fry for 3–4 minutes, turning frequently. Add chicken broth and leftover marinade. Cover and cook over low heat for about 20–30 minutes, checking and stirring occasionally. Chicken should be tender, and the sauce slightly thickened. Sprinkle with green onions. Serve hot or at room temperature.

Makes 20 wings and drumettes.

Lollipop Drumsticks

This is a very simple recipe, fun to make, popular at picnics and dinner parties. The lollipops are delicious hot or cold.

20 chicken wings

MARINADE FOR CHICKEN
1 heaping tablespoon fresh
   ginger, minced
3 cloves minced garlic
2 tablespoons green onion,
   minced
¼ cup soy sauce
¼ cup rice wine or dry sherry

Twist the joints of the chicken wings, push the skin and meat up around the thicker end, forming a lollipop shape. Separate that part from rest of wing and tip. Discard the tip. Rinse, drain and pat dry the lollipops and wings.

Combine the marinade ingredients in a large bowl. Marinate chicken for at least 3 hours, preferably overnight. Drain lollipops and wings from marinade and place on an aluminum-foil-lined baking pan. Bake at 350 degrees for 30–40 minutes. Place under broiler for a few minutes until brown.

Makes 20 lollipops and 20 wings.

Lotus Leaf Chicken

Lotus leaves are available in most Asian food markets, in large batches. They are approximately 12 inches in diameter.

1 pound glutinous rice,
   soaked overnight in cold
   water
4 large dried lotus leaves
1 whole chicken breast,
   boned, skinned, cut into
   ¾-inch pieces

Soak glutinous rice overnight, and cook according to directions. Cool until ready to use. Soak dried lotus leaves in warm water until soft and then dry with paper towels. Combine the marinade in a small bowl. Add chicken and marinate for 15–20 minutes. Soak mushrooms in hot water for 10 minutes; squeeze out excess water,

MARINADE FOR CHICKEN

1 tablespoon soy sauce
1 tablespoon rice wine or
  dry sherry
½ teaspoon white pepper
1 teaspoon sesame oil

OTHER INGREDIENTS

8 Chinese dried black
  mushrooms
3 tablespoons vegetable oil
1½ cup lean pork, cut
  coarsely into small pieces,
  sprinkled with 2 teaspoons
  soy sauce
⅔ pound medium-sized
  prawns, peeled, deveined,
  rinsed, and patted dry,
  coarsely chopped into
  small pieces
1 teaspoon rice wine or
  dry sherry
2 green onions, cut into ½-
  inch pieces
1 tablespoon soy sauce
1 tablespoon oyster sauce
2 teaspoons sesame oil
¼ cup chicken broth

remove and discard stems, and cut caps into thirds.

Heat wok with oil, swirling to coat sides. When smoky, add chicken and mushrooms and cook for 2 or 3 minutes, until chicken turns white. Remove from wok. Reheat, adding more oil only if wok looks dry. Add pork and stir-fry until color changes. Add prawns and wine, and cook until prawns turn pink. Add green onions, soy sauce, oyster sauce, and sesame oil, and mix well. Mix in rice, approximately 1 cup at a time, and blend all ingredients. Adjust amount of soy sauce and oyster sauce to taste. Add chicken broth to give the filling extra moisture.

TO FILL LOTUS LEAF:
Place ¼ of the filling in the center of a lotus leaf. Distribute the ingredients of the filling evenly for each of the leaves. There is a hole about ¾-inch wide in the center of the leaf, so cover it with filling and wrap another part of the leaf over it to secure. The leaves are big, usually 12 inches or wider in diameter, so this will be easy to do. Wrap the filling up and around into a 5-inch package, resembling a cross between a square and a rectangle. Place each seam side down on steam plate or rack. Steam in a wok over high heat for 15–20 minutes. Bring to serving table and cut a slit to open from top (keeps the contents hot) or unwrap and transfer filling to serving plate. It's more fun to eat it out of the lotus leaf.

Serves 4–6.

My Father's Chinese Deep-Fried Egg Puffs (Jah Donn)

When I was a little girl in Oakland's Chinatown, I used to go across the street from our restaurant to a coffee shop to buy these fried puffs. Years later, my father made them for our customers when we operated the Bamboo Hut restaurant in Hayward, California. I was always first in line to volunteer to taste test them. Substituting egg whites for whole eggs does not work well in this recipe.

2½ cups water
2 cups all-purpose flour
8 eggs
3 cups vegetable oil
1 cup white sugar

Bring water to a boil in a large pot. Stir in flour, a little at a time, mixing well with a whisk. Break the eggs in, one at a time, and continue to stir, until all 8 eggs are in the pot. This process takes approximately 10 minutes to form a batter.

Heat a wok or deep-fryer with vegetable oil to 360 to 375 degrees. Fill an ice cream scoop with the batter and gently place into the wok. Keep the jah donns from touching each other. Cook over medium-high heat for 10–12 minutes. The jah donns will burst gently. Drain the jah donns on a rack, and while they are still warm, roll them lightly in white sugar to coat.

Makes 10–12.

Popular Spring Rolls

Spring rolls, in some areas better known as Egg Rolls, are always popular with kids of all ages, and are on practically every Chinese restaurant menu. Now you can make them at home. They go well with Hot Mustard and Soy Sauce Dip or Hot Mustard and Catsup, separately or mixed together. For crispier spring rolls, allow to cool after initial cooking, then dip each one in basic deep-frying batter (see page 196), and deep-fry for another 4–5 minutes until golden brown.

FILLING

1 cup shredded cooked
   ham or Chinese-style roast
   pork
1 cup shredded cooked
   chicken breast
½ cup minced prawns or
   bay (cocktail) shrimp
4 Chinese dried black
   mushrooms
1 cup finely chopped celery
½ cup finely chopped
   bamboo shoots
2 cups fresh bean sprouts,
   coarsely chopped

OTHER INGREDIENTS

1 tablespoon vegetable oil
1 teaspoon sesame oil
1 tablespoon cornstarch
1 tablespoon soy sauce
1 teaspoon salt
1 pound spring roll wrappers
1 teaspoon cornstarch
1 egg, beaten, to seal spring
   rolls
3 cups vegetable oil for
   deep-frying

Soak mushrooms in warm water for 10 minutes, squeeze out excess water, remove and discard stems, and mince caps.

Heat a large wok with 1 tablespoon of oil, swirling to coat sides. Stir-fry the filling ingredients for 3–4 minutes over high heat. Add sesame oil, cornstarch, soy sauce, and salt. Remove from wok, place in a medium-sized bowl, cool for 20 minutes, and sprinkle with 1 teaspoon cornstarch.

To assemble spring rolls, place a heaping tablespoon of the filling in the center of a wrapper. Bring bottom of wrapper towards the top corner; bring sides together and roll. Seal with a splash of egg.

Heat a wok to 360 degrees with 3 cups of oil. Deep-fry the spring rolls for approximately 5 minutes, until golden brown. Drain and cool for 5 minutes. Cut into halves or thirds.

Makes 20.

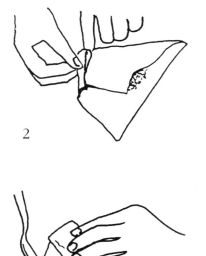

2

3

1

Potstickers

I prefer a non-stick pan to a cast iron pan to cook potstickers. Less oil is needed, and the potstickers slip out of the pan better. A quick way to prepare the filling is to crush the garlic and ginger in a food processor; add the cabbage and whirl it for a minute; then add the pork and green onion, and process for about 5 seconds. Transfer to a bowl and add remaining ingredients. Using a food processor saves time.

FILLING
½ pound lean ground pork
½ small head (approximately
   ½ pound) of napa cabbage,
   cored, finely chopped
1 green onion, minced
2 cloves garlic, minced
1 teaspoon fresh ginger,
   minced
1 tablespoon soy sauce
1 tablespoon rice wine or dry
   sherry
1 tablespoon cornstarch
1 teaspoon sesame oil
pinch of white pepper

OTHER INGREDIENTS
1 pound potsticker wrappers
4 tablespoons vegetable oil
2–3 cups chicken broth

TO PREPARE FILLING: chop the pork, cabbage, green onion, garlic, and ginger together. Place mixture into a large bowl, and add the soy sauce, wine, cornstarch, sesame oil, and white pepper. Refrigerate until ready to use.

TO ASSEMBLE POTSTICKERS: spoon 1 tablespoon of the filling into the center of each potsticker wrapper. Fold dough over to make a half-circle; moisten bottom half-circle with a small amount of water. Pleat edges firmly, forming 3–4 pleats on the top half-circle. Set each potsticker upright on a platter, so a flat base is formed.

Heat a large cast iron or non-stick pan. Add 2 tablespoons oil (with a non-stick pan, use 1 tablespoon oil). Place the pot-stickers close to one another, around the pan, but not touching. Brown the potstickers for about 30 seconds. Pour in enough broth to cover the potstickers half way. Cover and cook over moderate heat for 5 or 6 minutes. After the water evaporates, swirl in 1 teaspoon oil. Tip the pan to ease the potstickers out of the pan. Remove very carefully with a spatula. Turn each potsticker over, dark side up, and place on a platter to serve.

Serve potstickers, with an assortment of chili oil, vinegar, soy sauce, and sesame oil in little bowls. Mix to suit individual taste.

Makes 30.

Seafood Spring Rolls

This is a delicious spring roll for seafood lovers. The prawns and shrimp can be substituted with scallop, crab, or even lobster meat.

FILLING

4 Chinese dried black
  mushrooms
¾ cup prawns, peeled,
  deveined, minced
½ cup minced bay (cocktail)
  shrimp
1 cup finely chopped
  cabbage
1 cup bean sprouts,
  coarsely chopped

SEASONINGS

1 teaspoon sesame oil
1 tablespoon soy sauce
1 teaspoon salt
1 teaspoon rice wine or dry
  sherry
1 teaspoon white pepper

OTHER INGREDIENTS

1 tablespoon vegetable oil
1 tablespoon cornstarch
1 pound spring roll wrappers
1 egg, beaten (to seal spring
  rolls)
3 cups vegetable oil

Soak mushrooms in warm water for 10 minutes. Squeeze out excess water, remove and discard stems and mince caps. Combine filling ingredients in a medium-sized bowl.

Heat wok and add 1 tablespoon vegetable oil. Stir-fry the filling ingredients for 3–4 minutes. Add seasonings and mix well. Remove to a medium-sized bowl and cool for at least 20 minutes. Add cornstarch and mix well, so that the filling will hold together and not be watery.

To ASSEMBLE: place a heaping tablespoon of filling in the center of a wrapper. Fold over almost half way; bring sides together and roll into a cylinder. Seal with a little water. Heat a wok or large fry pan with 3 cups of vegetable oil to 360–375 degrees. Deep-fry each spring roll for approximately 5 minutes, until golden brown. Drain, let cool for 5 minutes. Cut into halves or thirds. Serve with hot mustard, or Hot Mustard and Soy Sauce Dip.

Makes approximately 12.

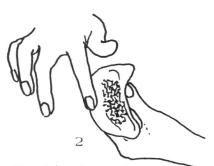

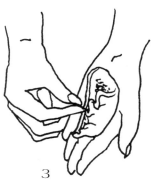

Potsticker Instructions

Simple Shrimp Toast

This is an excellent hors d'oeuvre or opening statement for a dinner party. May be prepared in advance, but fry the shrimp toast at the last minute.

6 slices of white or wheat
   bread, left out for 1–2 hours to
   dry
½ pound prawns peeled,
   deveined, and minced
¼ cup minced fresh or canned
   waterchestnuts
1 green onion, minced
½ teaspoon salt
½ teaspoon minced fresh
   ginger
1 egg white
1 tablespoon rice wine or dry
   sherry
dash of white pepper
1 teaspoon cornstarch
minced ham and parsley for
   garnish (optional)
2½ cups vegetable oil
Plum Sauce Dip (SEE RECIPE PAGE
   204).

Cut each slice of bread into 4 triangles, including crust.

Combine prawns, waterchestnuts, green onion, salt, ginger, egg, wine, pepper, and cornstarch in a medium-sized bowl. Scoop a heaping teaspoonful of mixture onto each triangle of bread. Spread and smooth out evenly. Place a pinch of minced ham on each piece, and top with a little parsley.

Add oil to wok and bring to medium high temperature, 350 degrees. When the oil is hot, gently place toast, shrimp side down, and fry for approximately 2 minutes. Turn and fry the other side for 30 seconds, until golden brown. Drain on paper towel. Serve with Plum Sauce Dip.

Makes 24.

Steamed Pork Buns (Cha Sil Bow)

This is the longest recipe in this cookbook, and may not be in keeping with my attempt to make recipes as easy as possible. But I have received so many requests that it just couldn't be omitted. Cha Sil Bows can be frozen. To reheat, simply steam for 15–20 minutes, or cover with plastic wrap and reheat in microwave oven for 1 minute, on high.

DOUGH

¼ ounce package active dry yeast

½ cup warm water (110 degrees F)

4 cups all-purpose flour

2 tablespoons lard

3 tablespoons sugar

1 cup milk

FILLING

1 tablespoon vegetable oil

2 cups minced Chinese-style roast pork

2 cloves fresh garlic, minced

½ cup green onions, minced

2 tablespoons hoisin sauce

2 tablespoons oyster sauce

1 tablespoon rice wine or dry sherry

2 tablespoons sugar

½ cup chicken broth

2 teaspoons cornstarch mixed well with 2 teaspoons water, to thin paste

½ teaspoon sesame oil

18–20 squares of waxed paper or parchment paper, cut into uniform, 2½-inch squares

DAY ONE: Place yeast in ½ cup of warm water for approximately 5 minutes, until it is completely dissolved, and begins to bubble. In a large mixing bowl, mix together flour, lard, sugar, and milk. Knead dough for 10 minutes. Work with it until it is smooth. If necessary, add a little flour if the dough is too sticky, or a little more milk if it is too dry. Form into a large ball and place the dough in a clean, large bowl. Cover with a cloth, and allow to rise overnight in a warm place, e.g., pre-heat oven at low setting for 2 minutes. Turn off heat, and place dough in. The warm spot on stove-tops above pilot light location is also a good source.

Prepare the filling by placing a small wok or frying pan over high heat for 1 minute. Add 1 tablespoon vegetable oil, and swirl around to coat evenly. Add roast pork, garlic, and green onions. Stir-fry for one minute. Stir in hoisin and oyster sauces, wine, sugar, and broth. Bring to a boil, and stir in cornstarch mixture. Season with sesame oil. Allow to cool. Refrigerate until ready to use.

DAY TWO: The dough has at least doubled in size by now. Place dough on a work surface that has been dusted with flour, and knead for 5 minutes. Cut into the center with a sharp knife. The dough should be smooth, with no bubbles, resembling soft cheese or tofu. Sprinkle a little more flour on the work surface. Break dough into 1½-inch to 2-inch balls. Flatten with the palm of your hand, and form a small well. Place 1 heaping teaspoon of filling into the center of the bun. Pinch the dough towards center, pleating and twisting to close. Place each bun, pleat side down, on a 2½-inch square of parchment or waxed paper. Allow to rise, uncovered, in a warm oven (pre-heated to warm, but shut off) for 15 minutes. Remove. Allow to rest at room temperature for 20 minutes.

To steam, place enough water in a 14-inch wok to come within 1 inch of the bottom of the steamer. Bring water to a boiling point. Have additional heated water on hand to replenish as necessary. Arrange pork buns on steamer rack(s), 1 inch apart. Cover, place steamer in the wok, and steam over high heat for 15 minutes.

Makes 18–20.

Tina's Onion Pancakes

This is a very simple recipe that my daughter Tina Dong developed. Onion pancakes make a good appetizer.

1 cup all-purpose flour
1/3 cup hot water
1/2 cup minced green onions
1/3 cup sesame seeds
extra all-purpose flour
2 tablespoons vegetable oil

Mix flour with water in a medium-sized bowl. Knead for 5 minutes. Add green onions and sesame seeds. Divide and form into 2-inch balls. Place on lightly-floured board and use a rolling pin to roll out 5-inch flat circles.

Heat a frying pan with 1 tablespoon of vegetable oil, swirling to coat entire bottom lightly. Fry pancakes over medium heat until lightly brown on both sides. Repeat procedure with remaining pancakes, adding a little oil to the pan if needed. Cut into quarters or sixths and serve as appetizer.

Makes approximately 10.

Tofu Fried Won Ton with Sweet and Sour Sauce

This is another recipe contributed by my friend Rhoda Wing. It sounded unusual enough to try, and I changed it just a little to suit my personal taste.

1 pound won ton wrappers
4 squares of firm tofu

FILLING
1 tablespoon fresh ginger, minced
2 tablespoons soy sauce
2 heaping tablespoons green onion, finely minced
½ teaspoon garlic, minced
1 tablespoon sesame oil

3 cups vegetable oil for deep-frying

SWEET AND SOUR SAUCE FOR TOFU WON TON
1 cup crushed pineapple, strawberries, or peaches
2 cups water
6 tablespoons honey
6 tablespoons cider vinegar
2 tablespoons cornstarch mixed with 2 tablespoons cold water

Crumble the tofu into small pieces with a fork. Squeeze the tofu dry with paper towel. Place in a medium-sized bowl and add filling ingredients. Hold a won ton wrapper in your hand so it resembles a diamond. Place a teaspoonful of filling near the center of won ton skin, and fold wrapper in twice towards you. Moisten the left corner with a small amount of water. Bring the right corner to the left corner and press the edges together to seal.

Heat oil in wok to 360–375 degrees. Fry one won ton to test the heat and adjust as necessary. Fry the won tons a few at a time until brown and crisp.

Place all sauce ingredients except the cornstarch in a saucepan and bring to a near boil. Stir frequently while cooking. Reduce heat, stir in cornstarch mixture and continue to cook until sauce thickens. Serve with won tons.

Makes 30–40.

Soups

Basic Chicken Broth

Basic Vegetarian Broth

Bean Curd Stick Soup

Bean Thread Soup

Chicken and Ginseng Soup

Chinese-Style Corn Soup

Hot 'n Sour Soup

Lions' Head Soup

Lotus Root Soup

Matrimony Vine Soup

Mongolian Fire Pot

Roast Duck Yee Foo Won Ton

Roast Pork Yee Foo Won Ton

Seafood Hot Pot

Simple Chinese Noodle Soup

Sizzling Rice Soup

Turkey Rice Congee

Watercress and Tofu Soup

Wintermelon Soup

Won Ton Soup

oup is an integral part of every Chinese meal. Simple or complex, it is always a welcome sight at a dining table. A whole meal can be in found in one soup bowl. For instance, a popular lunch for one person is an order of piping hot Won Ton Soup with a choice of toppings. I think it is especially comforting for a person who is under the weather to have a bowl of soup, whether it's rice congee, hot and sour, or won ton. It warms your tummy and your soul.

Our family dinners usually started off with a communal bowl of a simple vegetable soup (such as Chinese mustard greens) or a light, soothing herbal soup, which we drank with our Chinese soup spoons. If there was any leftover soup, we spooned it over our rice towards the end of the meal. At formal banquets, an elaborate soup may be presented in large, whole wintermelons with deft carvings of dragons and calligraphy on the exterior, or large oversized soup bowls are filled to the top, brimming with expensive shark's fin or birds' nest in a hearty chicken broth.

A soup is only as good as its base. It is crucial to start off with an excellent homemade chicken broth, or at least find a brand of canned broth most suitable for your palate. In today's quest for continual good health and longevity, I suggest making your own broth as often as possible, reducing the amount of salt used or buying low-sodium broth. See the first recipe in this section for more about making and storing a good basic broth.

Basic Chicken Broth

This is the basis of numerous soups, and is added to many stir-fry and other recipes for flavoring. You can vary the formula given here to suit your taste. Make chicken broth often as part of a food preparation routine. For example, as you bone a chicken, put the bones into the pot, along with trimmings, scrapings, and skins of vegetables such as onions, garlic, celery, cabbage, and carrots. All ingredients enhance the flavor of the broth.

A good way to keep chicken broth on hand is to freeze some in ice cube trays. After it is frozen, transfer 6 or 8 cubes to freezer bags. You will always have it on hand for its very frequent use in Chinese cooking.

1 whole chicken carcass or 2
  pounds chicken parts
8 cups cold water
1 small knob fresh Chinese
  ginger, crushed
1 whole yellow onion,
  quartered
2 stalks celery
2 green onions, cut to 1-inch
  pieces
salt to taste

Place the chicken in a large soup pot and add cold water to cover. Bring to a near boil, and lower heat. Add remaining ingredients and simmer at least 3 hours. Drain chicken and vegetables. Cool, refrigerate, and skim fat off top before use.

Makes 2 quarts.

Basic Vegetarian Broth

As with the Basic Chicken Broth described above, there are no exact ingredients. Experiment to find your favorite formula.

Simmer 2 pounds or more of a variety of vegetables and vegetable discards (e.g., bottom part of celery, peel from fresh ginger, shavings from carrot, green onions, bok choy) in 4 quarts of water for at least 3 hours. Ideas for vegetables: carrots, celery, turnips, potatoes, broccoli and cauliflower stems, mushroom stems, bok choy, green onion. Add small chunks of ginger and several cloves of mashed garlic, including the skins.

Simmer broth for at least 3 hours. Strain through a colander lined with cheese-cloth. Add soy sauce and other seasonings, such as sesame oil, after the broth is ready for use.

Makes 3 quarts.

Bean Curd Stick Soup

This is a classic, simple family-style soup. We enjoyed this soup throughout our youth, and I still enjoy making it.

2 cups bean curd stick, broken into 2-inch pieces
3 Chinese red dates, soaked in hot water for 10 minutes (no adequate substitute for these)
6 cups chicken broth

Break bean sticks and place in bowl or soup pot and pour in boiling water to soften. They will expand in size and turn white. Rinse with cold water and drain well. Bring chicken broth to boil in large saucepan.

2 teaspoons coarsely chopped
ginger
1 cup lean pork slices
1 tablespoon minced green
onion
1 tablespoon soy sauce
2 or 3 drops sesame oil

Add dates, ginger, and pork. Lower heat and cook for 10 minutes. Add bean curd stick, reduce heat, and simmer for 45 minutes.

Top with green onion and stir in soy sauce. Drizzle with a small amount of sesame oil.

Serves 5–6.

Bean Thread Soup

This is a simple recipe, combining packaged dried bean threads with a few ingredients. A good light lunch idea.

2 ounces dried bean threads
2–3 Chinese dried black
mushrooms
4 prawns, peeled, deveined,
and coarsely chopped
1 cup Chinese vegetables of
choice: bok choy, choy
sum, napa cabbage, snow
peas, or combinations of
each
4 cups chicken broth
1 teaspoon soy sauce
1 teaspoon green onion,
minced
⅛ teaspoon sesame oil

Soak bean threads in warm water until soft. Drain, and cut to 3-inch pieces.

Soak mushrooms in hot water for 10 minutes until soft. Squeeze out excess water, remove and discard stems, and slice caps into matchstick-sized pieces. Cut vegetables into 2-inch pieces.

Heat chicken broth in a large pot over medium heat. Add bean threads, mushrooms, prawns, and vegetables. Cook for 5 minutes.

Add soy sauce, top with minced green onions, and finish with sesame oil.

Serves 4–5.

Chicken and Ginseng Soup

I started to make this soup when I found out that ginseng helps the body cope with stress. Because of this, ginseng is beneficial for almost any ailment. Ginseng is an acquired taste for many people, but it makes a pleasant, soothing, and healthy addition to this recipe.

1 chicken, approximately 2½ pounds, cut into 8 parts, bone in, skin removed if desired
2 quarts chicken broth
6 Chinese dried black mushrooms
2 slices fresh ginger
6 Chinese red dates (optional)
4 or more pieces (medium size preferred) American ginseng roots
1 tablespoon green onion, minced
salt to taste

Soak mushrooms in hot water for 10 minutes. Squeeze out excess water, remove and discard stems, and cut caps into thirds.

Place chicken and chicken broth in large soup pot. Add mushrooms, ginger, dates, and ginseng. Cover and bring soup to a near boil, lower heat immediately, and simmer for an hour. Top with green onion. Flavor with salt to taste.

Serves 4–6.

Chinese-Style Corn Soup

This was frequently served at our restaurant, the Bamboo Hut in Hayward,
California, as "Soup of the Day." Use fresh, frozen or creamed corn—I prefer the
creamed corn because it gives the soup more texture and flavor.

1½ cups chicken
  breast (approximately
  2 medium-sized
  breasts), boned, skin
  removed, finely minced
1 egg white

SEASONING FOR CHICKEN
1 teaspoon rice wine or dry
  sherry
2 teaspoons soy sauce
1 teaspoon fresh ginger,
  finely minced
1 teaspoon tapioca starch
1 teaspoon sesame oil
½ teaspoon white pepper

OTHER INGREDIENTS
4 cups chicken broth
16½ ounce can creamed
  corn or 2 cups fresh or
  frozen corn
2 tablespoons minced
  Smithfield or any ham
  (optional)
1 egg or 2 egg whites,
  beaten
2 tablespoons cornstarch
  mixed well with 2 tablespoons cold water
1 teaspoon green onion,
  minced
sesame oil to taste

Place chicken in a large bowl and coat
with egg white. Add seasonings and mix
together. Set aside for 15 minutes.

Bring chicken broth to a boil in large
soup pot. Add corn and immediately stir
in the chicken. Continue stirring the
chicken rapidly to prevent minced
pieces from sticking together. Add ham,
and cook for about 1 minute, until
chicken turns white. Lower the heat and
gently swirl in beaten egg. Add cornstarch mixture and stir to thicken.

Top with green onions and more ham, if
desired. Drizzle with sesame oil.

Serves 4–5.

Hot and Sour Soup

Some gourmets judge a Chinese restaurant by the quality of its Hot and Sour Soup. It has a thick consistency, due to the addition of the cornstarch mixture. It is especially good if you feel a cold coming on, as it is hearty and robust.

6–8 cups chicken broth

4 Chinese dried black mushrooms

2–3 tablespoons rice or white vinegar

4 teaspoons soy sauce

1 tablespoon vegetable oil

½ cup finely shredded pork

⅛ cup cloud ear fungus

8–10 dried lily stems

½ cup bamboo shoots, cut into matchstick-sized pieces

2 tablespoons cornstarch mixed well with 2 teaspoons cold water

1 7-ounce block firm tofu cut into thin strips

2 eggs, beaten

1 teaspoon sesame oil

1 tablespoon ground white pepper

1 tablespoon green onion, minced

Place chicken broth in a large soup pot, and bring to near boil. Soak mushrooms in warm water for 10 minutes. Squeeze out excess water. Remove and discard stems. Cut caps into small pieces.

Heat wok with vegetable oil, swirling to coat sides. Stir-fry the pork, mushrooms, cloud ear fungus, lily stems, and bamboo shoots. Add 1 tablespoon soy sauce and stir-fry for a minute.

Transfer to soup pot. Add the vinegar and remaining teaspoon of soy sauce. Bring to a boil and stir in the cornstarch mixture until soup thickens. Add the tofu, and stir well. Remove pot from the heat. Swirl in beaten eggs. Add sesame oil and season with pepper. Sprinkle with minced green onion. Adjust flavor with more vinegar or pepper to suit individual taste.

Serves 6.

Lions' Head Soup

Lions' heads are big meatballs, simmered or baked until tender, and covered with napa cabbage. Cellophane noodles resemble a lion's whiskers. This is a very earthy, homestyle soup. I use my attractive Gourmet d'Expert electric cooker, made by Zojirushi, which holds almost three quarts when full, to cook and serve this soup. Use an electric cooker to free another burner on the stove.

6 Chinese dried black mushrooms

2 ounces dried cellophane noodles

1 pound lean ground pork

2 teaspoons fresh ginger

1 whole green onion, cut into 1-inch pieces

1 tablespoon young, fresh, or canned bamboo shoots

6 fresh or canned waterchestnuts, fresh preferred

2 tablespoons soy sauce

2 teaspoons rice wine or dry sherry

1 egg white

1/4 teaspoon white pepper

1 tablespoon cornstarch

1 tablespoon vegetable oil

1 teaspoon sesame oil

1 napa cabbage (approximately 3/4 pound) separated into 16 leaves uniform in size

4 cups chicken broth (includes 1/2 cup of liquid from soaking the mushrooms)

1 medium carrot cut into matchstick-sized pieces

1/2 cup onion, minced

1/4 cup ginger, minced

1/2 cup green onion, minced

Soak the mushrooms in hot water for 10 minutes. Drain excess water, reserving liquid to add to chicken broth, remove and discard stems, cut caps into halves.

While mushrooms are soaking, place cellophane noodles, with bands on, in a pot of boiling water to cover for 5 minutes. Cut in half and discard band. Drain and set aside.

Place pork, ginger, green onions, bamboo shoots, and waterchestnuts in a food processor and blend almost into a paste. Transfer to large mixing bowl. Add soy sauce, wine, egg whites, white pepper, and cornstarch. Mix well and form into 6 meatballs.

Heat a wok or electric cooker with 1 tablespoon oil, swirling to coat sides. Add 1/2 teaspoon sesame oil and gently cook 8 cabbage leaves for 30 seconds, being careful not to break the leaves. If electric cooker is not used, transfer cabbage leaves at this point to a heavy-duty casserole. Place meatballs on top. Add chicken broth. Place the carrots, black mushrooms, minced onion, and ginger on top. Cover with remaining cabbage leaves. Cover and simmer for 1 hour, until meatballs are tender.

During the last 15 minutes, add cellophane noodles to simmering liquid in casserole. Serve lions' head in the casserole. Drizzle with remaining 1/2 teaspoon sesame oil and top with minced green onion.

Serves 4–5.

Lotus Root Soup

Lotus root resembles links of raw potatoes. When sliced horizontally into circles, the pieces have patterns that resemble giant snowflakes. When bitten into, the lotus root is a little fibrous. I used to goof around and take a big bite, then pull on the lotus to let its fibers make whiskers around my mouth—not very ladylike. This makes a very delicious, hearty, family-style soup.

2 pounds fresh, firm lotus root
8 cups chicken broth
1 pound pork butt, excess fat removed, cut into 2-inch cubes
2 pieces of tangerine peel, softened in hot water
8 Chinese red dates, soaked in hot water
1 teaspoon salt
Chinese parsley (cilantro) sprigs

Peel and cut lotus root into rounds approximately ⅛-inch thick, and cut larger rounds into halves. Place pieces in a bowl of cold water immediately to avoid discoloration.

Put chicken broth in large pot, add lotus root, and bring to a boil. Lower heat, cover and cook for 30 minutes. Add the pork, tangerine peel, and dates and cook another 45 minutes. The lotus root and pork should be tender by now. Season with salt to taste. Top with Chinese parsley.

Serves 6–8.

Matrimony Vine Soup (Gow Gay Soup)

6 cups chicken broth
1 cup lean chicken meat, skinned and boned, cut into 1-inch pieces
1 teaspoon soy sauce
¼ teaspoon cornstarch
1 small piece of fresh ginger, the size of a quarter, mashed
1 pound matrimony vine (gow gay), stems removed and discarded
1 whole egg or two egg whites
½ teaspoon sesame oil

Heat chicken broth in large soup pot. Coat chicken pieces with soy sauce and cornstarch. Place ginger and chicken in broth. Cook over medium-low heat for 5 minutes. Add matrimony vine leaves and simmer for 10 more minutes. Stir in egg or egg whites, swirling them with a pair of chopsticks. Drizzle with sesame oil.

Serves 4–5.

Mongolian Fire Pot (Dai Bin Lo)

This is a relaxing and entertaining form of dining. The cooking is done at the table by you and your friends. The choices of food can vary according to your taste. The self-made soup is a perfect ending to an excellent and healthful meal.

½ pound beef flank, teriyaki-type thinly sliced against grain
1 chicken breast, boned and skinned
½ pound pre-cooked Chinese noodles

MARINADE FOR CHICKEN
2 tablespoons dry sherry or rice wine
2 tablespoons soy sauce
1 teaspoon fresh ginger, minced
1 clove garlic, minced

MARINADE FOR BEEF
1 tablespoon rice wine or dry sherry
1 teaspoon soy sauce
1 teaspoon minced fresh ginger
1 teaspoon sugar

OTHER INGREDIENTS
⅓ pound prawns
⅓ pound any type of fish filet, thinly sliced
2 cups bay or sea scallops, cut to bite-sized pieces
1 cup canned abalone, sliced into thin pieces
2 cups each of assorted vegetables, cut in bite-sized pieces, e.g., bok choy, spinach, bean sprouts, cabbage
2 cups tofu
2 quarts chicken broth
minced green onion to taste

SETUP
Each guest should have two rice bowls (one for uncooked food, the other to eat from), two pairs of chopsticks (one wooden set for cooking, another set for eating with), and a small food net. Before starting to cook, set out small dishes containing soy sauce, oyster and hoisin sauces, sesame oil, and chili paste to use as dips for cooked food.

Peel and devein prawns. Slice lengthwise in half. Rinse and pat dry.

Prepare chicken and beef marinades in 2 medium-sized bowls. Add meats to bowls and marinate for 2 hours.

Place a large electric skillet or firepot at the center of the table. Fill with broth, and maintain 400 degrees at all times while each person cooks his/her own food. Set individual dishes of the various food items around the skillet. At your leisure, cook a little of each of the ingredients. Use individual small food nets to place the food into the simmering broth to cook.

When the food is cooked, transfer it to individual bowls. When most of the food is consumed, place pre-cooked noodles into the broth in the skillet along with any leftover meat or vegetables to make the last course, a rich soup.

Serves 6–8.

Roast Duck Yee Foo Won Ton

6 Chinese dried black
  mushrooms
4 cups chicken broth
1 cup shredded napa cabbage
½ cup bamboo shoots, sliced
1 cup Chinese Roast Duck meat,
  minced
¼ cup fresh or frozen green peas
2 teaspoons cornstarch, mixed
  well with 2 teaspoons cold
  water
40 deep-fried won tons (SEE *Won
  Ton Soup* RECIPE PAGE 62)
2 green onions, minced
½ teaspoon sesame oil

Prepare fried won tons in advance. Soak mushrooms in warm water for 10 minutes. Remove and discard stems and mince caps. Bring chicken broth to boil in large soup pot. Add mushrooms, cabbage, and bamboo shoots, and cook for 3–4 minutes. Add duck meat and green peas. Swirl in cornstarch mixture slowly until soup thickens slightly. Stir in soy sauce. Add fried won tons, and top with green onions. Drizzle with sesame oil.

Serves 5–6.

Roast Pork Yee Foo Won Ton

This is a popular dish that requires cooking won ton twice. Fried won tons are tossed into a rich, tasty soup, with various toppings. It is one of my favorite dishes in Chinatown restaurants. For variety, substitute the roast pork in this recipe with ¼ cup each of cooked ham and cooked chicken, minced together. If desired, deep-fry ½ cup of fresh Chinese noodles, and add to the other ingredients.

40 fried won tons, prepared in advance (*Won Ton Soup* RECIPE P. 62)
8 cups chicken broth
1 cup fresh or frozen peas
½ cup or small can button
  mushrooms
3 egg whites, beaten
1 tablespoon cornstarch mixed
  well with 1 tablespoon cold
  water
1 tablespoon soy sauce
1 teaspoon sesame oil
½ cup Chinese roast pork, minced
1 green onion, minced

Heat chicken broth, peas, and mushrooms in a large soup pot. When soup comes to a boil, lower heat and add beaten eggs and stir for 15 seconds. Drop in the won tons. Bring soup back to boil. Add cornstarch mixture and stir until soup thickens. Adjust to desired thickness with more cornstarch and water. Season with soy sauce and sesame oil Sprinkle roast pork on top. Garnish with green onion.

Serves 6–8.

Seafood Hot Pot

This is an excellent alternative to the traditional Mongolian Fire Pot. Gather a few friends together and have a good time preparing this sea-sational dinner. Add any other seafoods not mentioned in recipe if desired: cleaned octopus, squid, sea cucumber, fish filet, fish cake—anything that is fresh and a favorite.

8 cups chicken broth
2 tablespoons rice wine or dry
   sherry
3 slices fresh ginger,
   sliced in 1-by-2-inch strips
1 fresh crab, cleaned; legs and
   joints cracked
8 tiger prawns, peeled, deveined, rinsed, and patted
   dry
8 Manila (or other favorite)
   clams in shell
8 sea scallops, cut into halves
   (or 16 bay scallops)
8 oysters of choice, shucked
chopped vegetables
1 pound pre-cooked Chinese
   egg noodles or bean threads
   or 2 cups pre-cooked rice

DIPPING SAUCE
1 tablespoon soy sauce
1 teaspoon fresh ginger,
   minced
2 teaspoons rice or white
   vinegar
½ teaspoon hot chili pepper oil
1 teaspoon sesame oil

SETUP
Each guest should have two rice bowls (one for uncooked food, the other to eat from), two pairs of chopsticks (one wooden set for cooking, another set to eat with), and a small food net.

Heat broth in a 14-inch electric wok or authentic Mongolian fire pot. Have all seafood and vegetables on hand. Allow your guests to pick and choose and cook their own meals. If you wish, offer individual strainer-spoons (usually gold-colored miniature "fish nets" made of wire) for diners to use to cook their chosen seafood. Add a variety of vegetables to the wok at your leisure. Add more broth as quantity diminishes. Afterwards, place noodles, bean threads, or rice into broth for self-made soup. Prepare dipping sauce by combining the soy sauce, ginger, vinegar, hot chili pepper oil, and sesame oil to taste.

NOTE: Use any assortment of napa cabbage, bok choy, mustard greens, fresh spinach, Shanghai bok choy, and Chinese broccoli, rinsed and chopped to 2–3-inch pieces, whole snow peas, cubes of bean cake—the possibilities are unlimited.

Serves 6–8.

Simple Chinese Noodle Soup

½ pound fresh Chinese
  noodles
2 Chinese dried black
  mushrooms
3 cups chicken broth
2 thin slices fresh ginger
1 tablespoon soy sauce
½ teaspoon sesame oil
½ cup cooked Chinese roast
  pork, cut into slivers, or
  ½ cup cooked chicken, cut
  into slivers
¼ cup green onion, finely
  minced
Chinese parsley (cilantro)
  sprigs

Place noodles in 4–5 cups of boiling water and cook for 2–3 minutes. Drain in a colander and rinse with cold water.

Soak mushrooms in hot water for 10 minutes, squeeze out excess water, remove and discard stems, cut caps into thin slices. Retain some of the mushroom soaking water to add to chicken broth.

Heat 3 cups of chicken broth in a large saucepan, adding some of the mushroom soaking water. Add slices of ginger and mushrooms and cook for 2 minutes. Return cooked noodles to pot, add soy sauce and sesame oil. Top with cooked roast pork or chicken, and sprinkle with green onion and Chinese parsley.

Serves 3–4.

Sizzling Rice Soup

Because it takes a few hours for the rice crust to dry properly, it should be prepared ahead of time. When I was a child, my parents purposely cooked rice until a brown crust formed around the bottom of the pot. After the rice was removed from the pot, water was added, along with a small amount of fermented bean curd for extra flavor before eating it, which was usually after dinner.

6 pieces of rice crust, broken
  into small parts
3 Chinese dried black
  mushrooms
5 cups chicken broth
½ cup cooked cocktail
  shrimp

To prepare rice crust, follow directions for preparing *Basic Steamed Rice*, (p.180) leaving a thin layer on bottom of pot. Leave the pot, uncovered, over pilot light or lowest heat until rice becomes dry—this takes a few hours. Remove in chunks and allow to sit until cool.

½ cup uncooked chicken, sliced in small pieces
½ cup sliced Chinese waterchestnuts
½ cup sliced bamboo shoots
¼ cup fresh or frozen green peas
2 teaspoons rice wine or dry sherry
½ teaspoon white pepper
sesame oil to taste
2 cups oil (to deep-fry rice)

Soak mushrooms in warm water for 10 minutes. Remove stems, squeeze out excess water, and slice caps into thin pieces. Place chicken broth in large soup pot, and bring to a rolling boil. Add mushrooms, shrimp, chicken, water chestnuts, bamboo shoots, and peas and cook for 2–3 minutes. Add wine, white pepper, and sesame oil. Transfer to serving tureen.

Heat 2 cups of oil in a wok or frying pan. Drop chunks of rice into oil and deep-fry for approximately 1 minute, until golden brown. Remove rice chunks and place on paper towel for a moment to absorb excess oil. Gently place chunks of rice into soup while they are still very hot.

Serves 5–6.

Turkey Rice Congee

This hearty soup—"jook"—is very traditional, served all over Asian communities from morning until night. You can substitute turkey with toppings of your choice, to be placed in soup pot during the last 20 minutes of cooking: minced roast duck, ground turkey or beef, chicken, raw fish filet, minced ham. A turkey carcass is perfect for jook. Add it to the soup pot, and remove when the jook is done.

1 cup long-grain rice
8 cups chicken broth
1 tablespoon fresh ginger, minced
2 green onions, minced
1 turkey thigh (approximately 2 pounds)
1 tablespoon soy sauce
1 teaspoon salt
1 teaspoon sesame oil

Rinse rice 2 or 3 times. Place rice, broth, ginger, and half of the green onions in a large soup pot and bring to a boil. Place turkey thigh in the pot, reduce heat, and simmer for 2–3 hours, stirring occasionally. The rice will eventually break down completely and the soup will become thick. Remove skin and bones from turkey thigh. Add soy sauce, salt, and drizzle with sesame oil and top with minced green onions.

Serves 6–8.

Watercress and Tofu Soup

This soup blends two mellow flavors, watercress and bean cake. When I'm in a hurry and happen to have these ingredients in the refrigerator, I cook up a pot of packaged dried noodles, substitute the seasoning packet with homemade or canned chicken broth, and top the soup with watercress and bean cake.

6 cups chicken broth
¼ pound lean pork, cut into matchstick-sized pieces
3 Chinese dried black mushrooms
4 cups fresh watercress, cut into 2-inch pieces
1 cup tofu, cut into ½-inch cubes
1 egg or 2 egg whites, beaten
1 teaspoon soy sauce
1 teaspoon sesame oil

Soak mushrooms in a bowl of hot water for 10 minutes. Squeeze out excess water, remove and discard stems, and cut caps into thirds. Place chicken broth in a large soup pot and bring to a boil. Reduce heat, add pork, and cook until pork changes color. Add mushrooms, watercress, and tofu. Cover and simmer for 5 minutes, until watercress wilts and turns bright green. Gently stir in beaten egg and season with soy sauce and sesame oil.

Serves 4–6.

Wintermelon Soup

Wintermelons are typically only available in Asian food markets, in sections or whole. Whole melons can weigh up to 20 pounds, and can last for several months after harvest. Cut-up pieces, will survive only a few days in the refrigerator. Wintermelons have thick, dark green, waxy skin, and white flesh which turns transparent during cooking. For special occasions, the whole melon shell doubles as a serving container. A good substitute for wintermelon is fuzzy melon (also known as fuzzy squash). Scrape fuzz from this melon before cooking, using a butter knife. For soup, cut the melon into thin, 1-inch lengths. If possible, use Virginia ham, which is considered closest in flavor to traditional Chinese ham.

1½ pound section of wintermelon
8 cups chicken broth
4 tablespoons minced cooked ham
½ cup minced cooked chicken
6 Chinese dried black mushrooms
6 fresh or canned waterchestnuts, thinly sliced
¼ cup fresh or frozen green peas
1 tablespoon rice wine or dry sherry
white pepper to taste
sesame oil
Chinese parsley (cilantro) for garnish

Soak mushrooms in warm water for 10 minutes. Squeeze out excess water, remove and discard stems, and dice caps.

To prepare wintermelon, remove rind, seeds, and fibrous part. Cut into ⅜-inch cubes or leave the rind on and cut into 1½-inch squares.

Place chicken broth in a large pot and bring to a boil. Add the wintermelon, 2 tablespoons ham, chicken, mushrooms, and waterchestnuts. Bring to a boil, stir for 1–2 minutes. Lower heat and let simmer covered for 20 minutes. Remove cover, add peas, and cook another 2–3 minutes. Add wine. Top with remaining 2 tablespoons minced cooked ham. Sprinkle with white pepper and drizzle with sesame oil. Garnish with Chinese parsley if desired.

NOTE: ¼ cup flaked crabmeat, cocktail shrimp, or minced lean pork can substitute for, or be added to ham and chicken.

Serves 8–10.

Won Ton Soup

I have yet to meet a person who doesn't like won ton. Won tons remind me of Italian raviolis and are delicious either in soup or fried. For fried won tons, use a small amount (¼ teaspoon) of filling, as cooking time is minimal.

WON TON WRAPPERS
1 pound won ton wrappers

WON TON FILLING
8 Chinese dried black
  mushrooms
⅓ pound lean ground pork
10 prawns, peeled, deveined,
  rinsed, and coarsely
  chopped
4 fresh or canned water-
  chestnuts, minced
1 green onion, minced
1 link of Chinese sausage (lob
  cheung), minced (optional)
1 egg
2 teaspoons soy sauce
1 teaspoon sesame oil

WON TON SOUP
6 cups chicken broth
1 cup sliced leftover meat
  such as cooked chicken or
  roast pork
1 cup bok choy or baby bok
  choy, cut to 1½-inch pieces
6–8 prawns, deveined, rinsed
½ cup sliced waterchestnuts
1 teaspoon soy sauce
½ teaspoon sesame oil
1 green onion, minced
1 tablespoon hot mustard
  powder, mixed with cold
  water to a paste

MAKE WON TONS
Soak mushrooms in warm water for 10 minutes. Squeeze out excess water. Remove and discard stems. Mince the caps. Save water used for soaking to add to broth. Use half of the mushrooms for filling, reserve other half for soup itself. Combine pork, prawns, minced waterchestnuts, green onion, and sausage on a chopping board. Chop all together with a cleaver. Place mixture in a medium-size bowl and add the egg, soy sauce, and sesame oil. Mix well.

Spoon a generous teaspoon of the filling in the center of won ton wrapper. Fold one corner over twice to form a triangle. Brush left side with a little of the filling. Bring the right side over, twisting slightly, so that the back of the right side meets the front of the left side.

Bring 8 cups of water to a boil in large pot. Add handfuls of prepared won tons and cook for approximately 4 minutes, until won tons float to the top. Remove won tons.

Add chicken broth and mushroom soaking liquid to soup pot and bring to boil. Add remainder of black mushrooms, bok choy, prawns, sliced waterchestnuts, or other desired toppings such as snow peas. Add won tons

to soup. Place roast pork on won tons right before serving, to retain the coating. Reduce heat and simmer as won tons are added.

Pour chicken broth and toppings over won tons, arranging the meat or chicken, and vegetables attractively. Add sesame oil and garnish with green onion. Add hot mustard and extra soy sauce to taste, or have on hand for diners.

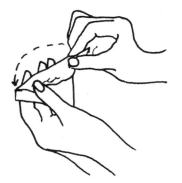

NOTE: For Fried Won Tons, heat 3 cups of vegetable oil in a wok or fry pan to 350 degrees. Deep-fry won tons, a handful at a time, until golden brown. Remove and drain on absorbent towels.

Serves 4–6.

Seafood

Abalone with Black Mushrooms and Lettuce

Broccoli Prawns

Chinese Fish Fry

Chinese-Style Paella

Clams with Black Bean Sauce

Classic Prawns with Black Bean Sauce

Crab Cantonese

Crab Meat and Eggs

Curried Prawns

Curried Prawns Rice Noodles (Chow Fun)

Filet of Fish with Broccoli

Filet of Rock Cod with Vegetables

Filet of Sole in Brown Bean Sauce

Fried Tiger Prawns

Ginger Crab

Kung Pao Prawns

Prawns with Tofu

Scallop and Prawn Stir-Fry

Simple Steamed Whole Fish

Steamed Salmon Steaks

Steamed Whole Sand Dab

Stir-Fried Bittermelon with Prawns

he word for fish in Chinese sounds like the word for abundance. Fish symbolizes good fortune, and is always served at dinner parties and banquets. It is a tradition to have the fish head face the guest of honor, and to serve the best part of the fish to him or her— that is, the cheek part of the fish head. My good friend Chef Martin Yan and I once had dinner in a Chinese restaurant in San Francisco's Chinatown. We ordered our favorite menu, a bowl of Chinese watercress soup, a dish of stir-fried, plain fresh bok choy, and a whole steamed fish. When the fish came to our table, Martin served the cheek to me, and I tried to reciprocate by serving the other cheek to him.

Fish is nutritious and usually low in saturated fat. Freshness is of course very crucial (choose one from a fish tank if you can). The simpler the preparation, the more healthful the fish. The best way to cook fish is to steam it, and to splash a small amount of hot oil and minced green onion on top right before serving. Another traditional cooking method is to steam a whole or filets of fish with fermented black bean sauce and ginger. This sauce is so good with sea food, and many of the recipes in this section call for it. Fresh fish is plentiful in most areas of the United States, so take advantage of the opportunity to enjoy many different kinds, such as flounder, rock cod, halibut, black bass, and salmon, to name a few.

Besides fish, the Chinese are fond of prawns, crabs, lobsters, clams, oysters, and mussels, all with due respect worthy of these treasures from the sea.

Abalone with Black Mushrooms and Lettuce

Canned abalone is an acceptable and delicious substitute for fresh abalone in this classic Chinese banquet dish and popular entrée for dinner parties.

12 high-quality Chinese
   dried black mushrooms
1 head iceberg lettuce,
   shredded
3 cups chicken broth
1 tablespoon vegetable oil
1 green onion, cut into 1-inch
   pieces
2 cloves garlic, finely minced
1 cup thin slices of abalone
1 tablespoon oyster sauce
1 teaspoon soy sauce
1 teaspoon cornstarch mixed
   well with 2 teaspoons cold
   water
1 teaspoon sesame oil

Soak mushrooms in hot water for 10 minutes. Squeeze out excess water. Remove and discard stems. Leave caps whole. Blanch lettuce in 3 cups of boiling chicken broth or combination of broth and water for 1 minute. Transfer to a serving platter and cover.

Heat wok with oil, swirling to coat sides. Stir-fry the onion, garlic, and mushrooms for 2–3 minutes over medium heat. Add ½ cup chicken broth, cover and cook for 5–6 minutes, until most of the broth has evaporated. Add the abalone and stir over high heat for 1 minute. Add another ½ cup chicken broth, oyster and soy sauces. Bring to a boil, and add cornstarch mixture, stirring until sauce thickens slightly. Drizzle with sesame oil and arrange abalone and mushrooms over precooked lettuce.

Serves 2–3.

Broccoli Prawns

To feature attractively, line serving platter with broccoli florets and place prawns in the center.

2 teaspoons vegetable oil

1 pound broccoli florets and tender parts of stems, trimmed and sliced diagonally into thin 1½-inch pieces

2 slices fresh ginger approximately 2 by 2 inches, cut to matchstick-sized pieces

½ pound medium-sized prawns, peeled, deveined, rinsed, and patted dry

BLACK BEAN SAUCE
SEE RECIPE *Master Black Bean Sauce* PAGE 201.

OTHER INGREDIENTS
¾ cup chicken broth
¼ teaspoon sugar
1 teaspoon soy sauce
1 tablespoon cornstarch mixed well with 2 tablespoons cold water

Heat wok with oil, swirling to coat sides. Cook broccoli over high heat for 2–3 minutes. Add a small amount of chicken broth, and cook until broccoli turns bright green. Transfer to plate.

Reheat wok, add another teaspoon of oil, swirling to coat sides. Add ginger and prawns, and cook until prawns begin to turn pink. Mix in black bean sauce. Return broccoli to wok, add chicken broth, sugar, and soy sauce. Bring to boil and gradually stir in cornstarch mixture. Continue to cook until sauce thickens slightly.

Serves 2–3.

Chinese Fish Fry

Trout or similar fish may be substituted for the flounder in this recipe.

1 whole flounder, approximately 2 pounds

MARINADE FOR FISH
1 tablespoon rice wine or dry sherry
2 teaspoons minced fresh ginger
splash of soy sauce
½ teaspoon white pepper

OTHER INGREDIENTS
3 cups vegetable oil for deep-frying
2 egg whites, beaten
½ cup flour
¼ cup cornstarch
2 tablespoons minced green onions
2 tablespoons rice wine or dry sherry
1 tablespoon soy sauce
Chinese parsley (cilantro)

Rinse fish, remove scales, gills, and innards and pat dry with paper towel. Cut deep gashes into thick part of the body of the fish. Place fish in a deep dish, coat with marinade ingredients, and marinate for at least 30 minutes.

Heat oil in wok. Test readiness of oil for deep-frying by placing a wooden chopstick in center of wok—if oil bubbles around the chopstick, the oil is ready. Be sure fish is dry. Coat the fish with beaten egg white, flour, and cornstarch. Shake off excess flour. Gently place the fish in the wok and cook over high heat until golden brown and crispy, approximately 15 minutes. Remove and place on paper-towel-lined plate to drain oil. Transfer to warm serving platter.

Heat a second wok or saucepan with 1 teaspoon of oil, cook green onion and add wine and soy sauce. Drizzle over fish. Garnish with Chinese parsley.

Serves 2–3.

Chinese–Style Paella

I have prepared this numerous times for dinner parties. It is quite time-consuming, but we have many friends who are as crazy as my husband and I are about seafood. If desired, add Chinese or Italian sausage.

---

2 chicken legs and thighs, excess fat removed, chopped into 2-inch pieces, with bone in
2½ cups long-grain rice

MARINADE FOR CHICKEN
1 tablespoon soy sauce
1 teaspoon fresh ginger, minced
2 teaspoons rice wine or dry sherry
2 cloves garlic, minced
1 teaspoon cornstarch

OTHER INGREDIENTS
8 Chinese dried black mushrooms
1 tablespoon vegetable oil
2 medium yellow onions, thinly sliced
¼ pound cooked ham, cut in 1-inch cubes
2 green onions cut to 1-inch pieces + 1 tablespoon minced green onion
pinch of powdered saffron
1½ cups chicken broth
½ pound fresh halibut, cut in 1-inch cubes
8 of your favorite type of clams
8 mussels, scrubbed clean

Mix marinade ingredients in a large bowl. Add chicken and marinate for 2 hours. Soak mushrooms in hot water for 10 minutes; squeeze out excess water, remove and discard stems, and leave caps whole.

Place rice in a pot and add enough cold water to cover rice. Stir the rice with your hand; the water will become milky. (Washing the rice removes excess starch and prevents cooked rice from being gummy.) Pour the water out of the pot carefully. Repeat until the water runs clear. Fill pot with water to approximately ¾ inch above rice level. Cover and place over high heat. When the water boils rapidly, reduce heat to lowest setting and simmer while preparing other ingredients.

While the rice is cooking, heat a 14-inch wok with oil, swirling to coat sides. Remove chicken from marinade and brown it on all sides. Transfer to serving platter. Reheat wok, adding a little more oil if necessary. Stir-fry the onion, mushrooms, ham, and 1-inch pieces of green onion for 3–4 minutes. Return chicken to wok and stir. Place the mixture on top of the cooking rice and sprinkle with saffron. Add chicken broth gradually and stir to mix well.

Evenly distribute all seafood on top,

12–16 tiger prawns, peeled, deveined, rinsed, and sprinkled with a small amount of rice wine or dry sherry

1 whole cooked crab, separated and cracked

¾ cup frozen or fresh green peas or 12 fresh snow peas

1 teaspoon sesame oil

leaving clams and mussels closer to top so you can watch for them to open up. Cover and cook for about 20 minutes, until clams and mussels open. Discard any that do not open. Stir in green peas or snow peas, minced green onion, and mix everything together. Drizzle with sesame oil.

Serves 6–8.

Clams with Black Bean Sauce

The chili paste in this recipe is usually sold in Asian specialty shops, in jars. Substitute any kind of chili paste that is available. For less spice, reduce amount, or eliminate the chili paste, and increase amount of fermented black bean sauce. Note: fresh live clams are closed shut. Clams that do not open after cooking should be discarded.

1½ pounds live clams (approximately 24)—succulent Manila clams are recommended

BLACK BEAN SAUCE
1½ tablespoons fermented black beans, rinsed and drained

3 cloves garlic, minced

1 tablespoon soy sauce

1 tablespoon rice wine or dry sherry

½ teaspoon sugar

OTHER INGREDIENTS
1 tablespoon vegetable oil

1 inch slice fresh ginger, peeled and mashed

1 teaspoon chili paste

½ cup chicken broth

1 green onion, cut to 1-inch pieces

2 teaspoons cornstarch mixed well with 1 tablespoon cold water

Most clams are clean at the time of purchase, but scrubbing the shells is recommended. Discard any that are open.

Prepare the black bean sauce by placing black beans and garlic in a small bowl, and mashing them together with the end of a cleaver. Stir in soy sauce, wine, and sugar. Set aside.

Place wok over high heat until hot. Add vegetable oil, swirling to coat sides. When the oil is smoky, add the clams, ginger, and black bean sauce. Stir-fry over high heat for 2 minutes.

Add remaining ingredients except for green onion and cornstarch mixture. Cover and cook for 3–4 minutes, until all the clam shells open. Add green onions and cornstarch mixture and stir gently until sauce thickens.

Classic Prawns with Black Bean Sauce

For added color, substitute half of the green bell pepper in this recipe with red or yellow ones, or a combination of all three.

1 tablespoon vegetable oil
⅓ pound lean ground pork
1 yellow onion, cut into medium-sized chunks
1 pound prawns, peeled, deveined, rinsed, and patted dry

BLACK BEAN SAUCE
2 tablespoons fermented black beans, rinsed and drained
2 cloves garlic, minced
1 tablespoon soy sauce
1 teaspoon rice wine or dry sherry
½ teaspoon sugar

OTHER INGREDIENTS
1 green bell pepper, cut into medium-sized chunks
1 cup chicken broth
1 tablespoon cornstarch mixed well with 2 teaspoons cold water
2 eggs or 1 egg and 2 egg whites, beaten
1 tablespoon minced green onions

Prepare the black bean sauce: place the fermented black beans and garlic in a small bowl and mash together to a pulp with end of cleaver. Stir in soy sauce, wine, and sugar.

Heat wok with oil, swirling to coat sides. Over high heat, stir-fry the pork until it changes color. Add the onion, prawns, and black bean paste. Stir-fry for 2 minutes until prawns begin to turn pink. Add bell pepper chunks and broth, and bring to a boil. Gently stir in the cornstarch mixture and cook until sauce thickens. Lower heat. Swirl in beaten eggs, and top with minced green onions.

Serves 3–4.

Crab Cantonese

For added color, substitute the green bell pepper in this recipe with a red or yellow one, or a combination of all three.

1 large fresh crab (approximately 3 pounds), cleaned, chopped, and cracked
⅓ pound lean ground pork

BLACK BEAN PASTE
2 tablespoons fermented black beans, rinsed and drained
2 cloves garlic, minced
1 tablespoon soy sauce
1 teaspoon rice wine or dry sherry
½ teaspoon sugar

OTHER INGREDIENTS
1 tablespoon vegetable oil
1 yellow onion, cut into 1-inch chunks
1 green bell pepper, cut into 1-inch chunks
1 teaspoon soy sauce
1 cup chicken broth
1 tablespoon cornstarch mixed well with 2 teaspoons cold water
2 eggs, beaten
2 tablespoons green onion, minced

Prepare the black bean paste: place black beans and garlic in a small bowl and mash together to a pulp with the end of a cleaver. Add soy sauce, wine, and sugar.

Heat wok with vegetable oil, swirling to coat sides. Over high heat, stir-fry the pork until pink color disappears. Add the onion, black bean paste, and crab. Stir-fry for 3–4 minutes; add the bell pepper, soy sauce, and chicken broth and stir for 2–3 minutes. When broth begins to boil, stir in the cornstarch mixture until the sauce thickens slightly. Turn off heat, and swirl in eggs. Top with green onion.

Serves 3–4 as a side dish.

Crab Meat and Eggs

2 teaspoons vegetable oil
1 teaspoon minced fresh
  ginger
2 cloves garlic, minced
2 Chinese dried black
  mushrooms
7 ounces fresh or canned
  crabmeat
1 teaspoon rice wine or dry
  sherry
1 tablespoon minced green
  onion
4 eggs or 2 eggs and 3 egg
  whites, beaten
¼ teaspoon salt
¼ teaspoon white pepper

Soak mushrooms in hot water for 10 minutes. Squeeze out excess water, remove and discard stems, and mince caps.

Heat wok with oil, swirling to coat sides. Add ginger, garlic, and black mushrooms. Cook over high heat until aromatic. Add crab meat, wine, and green onion and stir-fry over high heat for 1 minute. Stir in beaten eggs and when they begin to whiten and stiffen, turn over to fry the other side. Season with salt and white pepper.

Serves 2–3.

Curried Prawns

2 tablespoons vegetable oil
1 yellow onion, sliced thinly
2 slices of fresh Chinese
  ginger, approximately 1 by 2
  inches, sliced to matchstick
  size pieces
1 green bell pepper (or for
  added color, ½ green and ½
  red bell pepper)
1 pound medium or large tiger
  prawns, peeled, deveined,
  rinsed, and patted dry
2 tablespoons curry powder
½ teaspoon sugar
1 teaspoon soy sauce
½ cup chicken broth
1 teaspoon cornstarch mixed
  well with 2 teaspoons cold
  water
1 teaspoon sesame oil

Heat wok with tablespoon of oil, swirling to coat sides. Stir-fry onion, ginger, and bell pepper for a few minutes until onion is translucent. Remove and set aside.

Reheat wok, add remaining oil, swirling to coat sides. Stir-fry prawns over high heat until they turn pink. Add curry, sugar, soy sauce, and chicken broth. Return vegetables to wok. Bring to a boil, stir in cornstarch mixture, and cook until sauce thickens. Drizzle with sesame oil. Serve over rice or noodles.

Serves 3–4.

Curried Prawns Rice Noodles (Chow Fun)

½ pound medium-sized
  prawns, shelled, deveined,
  rinsed and patted dry
2 tablespoons vegetable oil
1 yellow onion, thinly sliced
2 cloves garlic, minced
4 strips of rice noodles, cut
  into 1-by-1½-inch pieces

MARINADE FOR PRAWNS
1 teaspoon rice wine or dry
  sherry
1 teaspoon soy sauce
½ teaspoon white pepper

OTHER INGREDIENTS
½ red bell pepper, sliced into
  matchstick-sized pieces
1 heaping teaspoon curry
  powder
½ cup bean sprouts
1 green onion, cut into 1-inch
  pieces
½ teaspoon sesame oil
chili pepper oil (optional)
Chinese parsley sprigs
  (cilantro)

Mix marinade ingredients in a large
bowl. Add prawns and marinate for 30
minutes.

Heat wok with 1 tablespoon vegetable
oil. When oil begins to smoke, stir-fry
prawns for 2–3 minutes until they begin
to turn pink. Remove from wok.

Reheat wok and add another tablespoon
of oil. Stir-fry onion, garlic, and rice
noodles until onion becomes translucent
and the rice noodles brown. Return
prawns to wok, add red bell pepper, and
continue to stir-fry. Add the curry powder, using more or less to suit your taste.
Toss in the bean sprouts and green
onions. Stir-fry 1–2 minutes until bean
sprouts are cooked. Drizzle in sesame
oil, and season with chili oil, if desired.
Garnish with Chinese parsley.

Serves 5–6.

Filet of Fish with Broccoli

¾–1 pound filet of sea bass
   or similar fish

MARINADE FOR FISH
1 tablespoon rice wine or dry
   sherry
1 teaspoon soy sauce
½ teaspoon salt
sprinkle of cornstarch

OTHER INGREDIENTS
¾ pound (or a medium-
   sized bunch) fresh
   broccoli
3 teaspoons vegetable oil
4 slices fresh ginger, cut into
   thin slices
¾ cup chicken broth
1 teaspoon cornstarch mixed
   well with 2 teaspoons cold
   water
⅛ teaspoon white pepper
sesame oil to taste
½ cup minced green onion

Mix together the marinade ingredients in a large bowl. Cut fish into 2-inch strips and marinate for at least 30 minutes.

To prepare broccoli, keep small florets whole, slice larger ones vertically into halves or quarters. Trim tough part of stem, and slice remaining stems diagonally into 1-inch long pieces.

Heat wok with 2 teaspoons oil, swirling to coat sides. Stir-fry half of ginger and all broccoli over high heat for 2–3 minutes; add ½ cup chicken broth and continue to cook until broccoli turns bright green. Remove ingredients from wok and wipe wok dry.

Reheat wok with remaining teaspoon oil. Add 2 slices of ginger and cook until fragrant. Add marinated fish and cook for 3–4 minutes until color of fish changes. Return broccoli to wok, add remaining ¼ cup broth and cornstarch mixture, and cook until sauce thickens slightly. Drizzle with white pepper and sesame oil; top with minced green onions.

Serves 2–3.

Filet of Rock Cod with Vegetables

Red snapper or halibut are suggested substitutes for rock cod.

1 pound filet of rock cod
4 Chinese dried black
   mushrooms
1 pound broccoli, or ½ pound
   broccoli and ½ pound
   cauliflower
1 tablespoon vegetable oil
½ yellow onion, cut to thin
   slices

BLACK BEAN SAUCE
1 tablespoon fermented black
   beans, rinsed and drained
2 cloves fresh garlic, minced
1 teaspoon rice wine or dry
   sherry
1 teaspoon soy sauce
½ teaspoon sugar

OTHER INGREDIENTS
1 cup chicken broth
1 tablespoon cornstarch mixed
   well with 2 tablespoons cold
   water

Soak mushrooms in hot water for 10 minutes. Squeeze out excess water, remove and discard stems, and slice caps into matchstick-sized slivers.

Trim stems of broccoli and/or cauliflower, and slice diagonally into 1-inch pieces. Cut florets into bite-sized pieces.

Blanch vegetables in a large pot of boiling water for 3–4 minutes, until broccoli turns bright green. Drain and set aside.

Place black beans and garlic in a small bowl and mash together with the end of a cleaver. Stir in soy sauce, wine, and sugar.

Heat wok with oil, swirling to coat sides. Add onion and mushrooms and stir-fry until onion is translucent. Add the fish and fermented black bean sauce and stir-fry over high heat for 2–3 minutes, or until fish turns white. Stir in chicken broth, return vegetables, and mix thoroughly.

Form a well in the middle of the wok and stir in cornstarch mixture, cooking until sauce thickens. Adjust sauce by adding more cornstarch if necessary.

Serves 2–3.

Filet of Sole in Brown Bean Sauce

Serve this fish on a bed of shredded lettuce for an attractive presentation.

4 filets of sole, sand dab,
  flounder, or rex sole
¼ cup all-purpose flour
white pepper

BROWN BEAN SAUCE
1 teaspoon fresh ginger,
  minced
2 teaspoons soy sauce
1 tablespoon brown bean
  sauce (min see sauce)
2 teaspoons rice wine or dry
  sherry
¼ cup chicken broth
2 teaspoons cornstarch mixed
  well with 1 teaspoon cold water

OTHER INGREDIENTS
1 cup vegetable oil for deep-
  frying
1 green onion (gently mash
  white part with side of cleaver,
  then slice into thin slivers)

Dust filets of fish with flour and pepper.

In a small saucepan, heat ginger, soy sauce, brown bean sauce, wine and chicken broth. Add cornstarch mixture and cook until sauce thickens.

Add oil to wok and heat to 350 degrees. Gently place the fish in the wok and deep-fry for 4–5 minutes until brown. Remove and drain on paper towels and place on serving platter. Pour sauce over fish and top with green onions.

Serves 2–3.

Fried Tiger Prawns

If tiger prawns are not available, use any type of available fresh medium to large-size prawns. These are excellent as an appetizer or first course, served with hot mustard and soy sauce dip.

1 pound uncooked, shelled
  tiger prawns, deveined,
  washed, and patted dry

Heat wok or electric wok to 375 degrees. Test oil with a bamboo chopstick for readiness. If bubbles appear around

3 cups vegetable oil
salt

Basic Deep-Fry Batter (SEE RECIPE PAGE 196)

the chopstick, the oil is ready. Dip each prawn in the batter and gently place into hot oil. Cook for approximately 3 minutes each side (check occasionally) until golden brown. Drain on paper towels and sprinkle with salt to taste.

Serves 3–4

Ginger Crab

1 fresh crab (approximately 3 pounds), cleaned, chopped, and cracked
2 tablespoons rice wine or dry sherry
3 tablespoons flour

GINGER SAUCE
1 heaping tablespoon fresh ginger, minced
½ cup chicken broth
2 teaspoon rice wine or dry sherry
1 tablespoon soy sauce
½ teaspoon sesame oil

OTHER INGREDIENTS
3 cups vegetable oil, for deep-frying
1 whole green onion
2 slices of fresh ginger, approximately 1 by 2 inches, cut to matchstick-sized pieces
2 teaspoons cornstarch mixed with 1 tablespoon cold water
white pepper
Chinese parsley (cilantro) sprigs

Combine the crab and wine and let stand for 10–15 minutes. Dust pieces of crab lightly with flour.

Combine ginger sauce ingredients in a small bowl and set aside.

Heat vegetable oil in wok to 350 degrees for deep-frying. Add crab and cook for 2–3 minutes until a light crust forms around the edges. Remove and drain well.

Gently mash the white part of the green onion with side of cleaver. Cut green part into 1-inch pieces.

In a clean wok, add oil, swirling to coat sides. Stir-fry ginger and green onion for 1 minute. Return crab to wok; pour in the ginger sauce, cover, and cook over high heat for 5–6 minutes. Stir in the cornstarch mixture, and cook until sauce thickens slightly. Sprinkle with white pepper. Top with generous garnish of Chinese parsley.

Serves 3–4 as a side dish.

Kung Pao Prawns

Once all the ingredients are in place, this hot and spicy dish is cooked up in a matter of minutes. This is a northern-style stir-fry, excellent over rice or noodles, or as a main course.

---

²⁄₃ pound fresh prawns,
peeled, shelled, deveined,
rinsed, and patted dry with a
towel
1 egg white
1 teaspoon soy sauce
1 teaspoon rice wine or dry
sherry
½ teaspoon white pepper

SEASONING SAUCE
2 cloves crushed garlic
2 tablespoons soy sauce
1 teaspoon oyster sauce
1 teaspoon rice wine or dry
sherry
½ cup chicken broth

OTHER INGREDIENTS
2 tablespoons vegetable oil
4–5 dried red chili peppers
1 yellow onion, thinly sliced
1 green bell pepper, diced into
½-inch pieces
¼ cup sliced bamboo shoots
2 green onions, cut to 1-inch
pieces
½ cup roasted unsalted peanuts
1 tablespoon cornstarch mixed
with 2 tablespoons cold
water
½ teaspoon sesame oil

Place prawns in a bowl and toss with egg white, soy sauce, wine, and white pepper.

Prepare the seasoning sauce: mix ingredients and set aside.

Heat wok with oil, swirling to coat sides. When the wok is very hot, stir-fry the chili peppers until they are black, and remove and set aside. Immediately add the yellow onion, prawns, bell pepper, bamboo shoots, and green onions. Stir-fry for 30 seconds, until yellow onion turns translucent and prawns change color. Add the season-ing sauce. Stir-fry for 30 seconds. Add peanuts. Stir in cornstarch mixture and cook until sauce thickens slightly. Sprinkle with sesame oil. Stir to heat through.

Serves 3–4.

Prawns with Tofu

Add 2 cups cooked broccoli or other favorite green vegetable to this dish for extra flavor and color.

½ pound medium-sized prawns, peeled, and de-veined, rinsed, and patted dry
3 Chinese dried black mushrooms

MARINADE FOR PRAWNS
1 teaspoon fresh ginger, finely minced
1 teaspoon rice wine or dry sherry
sprinkle of soy sauce

OTHER INGREDIENTS
1 tablespoon vegetable oil
2 slices of fresh ginger, ap-proximately 1 by 2 inches, cut into thin slivers
½ cup green onions, cut into ½-inch pieces
2 cups of firm tofu, cut into 1-inch cubes
2 tablespoons oyster sauce
1 teaspoon soy sauce
1 cup chicken broth
1 tablespoon cornstarch mixed with 1½ tablespoons cold water
½ teaspoon sesame oil
sprinkle of white pepper
½ cup minced green onion

Soak mushrooms in hot water for 10 minutes. Squeeze out excess water; remove and discard stems, and cut caps into thin pieces.

Place prawns in a small bowl and toss with marinade ingredients. Marinate for 30 minutes.

Heat wok with oil, swirling to coat sides. Stir-fry prawns over high heat until they turn pink. Remove from wok.

Reheat wok, adding a little more oil only if sides look dry. Stir-fry ginger, mush-rooms, and green onions for 1 minute. Stir in tofu, oyster and soy sauces, cover and cook for 2–3 minutes. Add chicken broth, bring to a boil and stir in corn-starch mixture. Cook until sauce thick-ens slightly.

Return prawns to wok and and stir to blend with other ingredients. Drizzle with sesame oil and sprinkle with white pepper. Top with green onion.

Serves 2–3.

Scallop and Prawn Stir-Fry

⅓ pound sea scallops, cut into halves

½ pound medium-sized or tiger prawns, peeled, deveined, rinsed, and patted dry

BLACK BEAN SAUCE

2 tablespoons fermented black beans

1 teaspoon ginger, minced

3 cloves garlic, minced

1 tablespoon rice wine or dry sherry

1 teaspoon soy sauce

OTHER INGREDIENTS

1 tablespoon vegetable oil

1 heaping teaspoon minced garlic

1 yellow onion, cut into small chunks

1 whole green bell pepper, cut into 1-inch-square chunks

1 cup chicken broth

1 tablespoon cornstarch mixed with 1½ tablespoons cold water

1 tablespoon soy sauce

1 tablespoon minced green onion

Prepare black bean sauce: Place black beans, garlic, and ginger in a small bowl and mash together to a pulp with the end of a cleaver. Add wine and soy sauce.

Heat wok with oil, swirling to coat sides. When smoky, stir-fry onion and minced garlic until onion becomes translucent.

Add scallops and prawns and cook over high heat, mixing in black bean sauce.

Add bell pepper. Cook for 2–3 minutes. Add chicken broth and bring to boil.

Gradually add cornstarch mixture and continue to cook until sauce thickens. Add soy sauce, mix through, and top with minced green onion.

Serves 4.

Simple Steamed Whole Fish

1 whole fresh fish (approximately 2 pounds) sea bass, rock cod, or flounder

TOPPING FOR FISH
1 tablespoon soy sauce
1 teaspoon salt
2 teaspoons rice wine or dry sherry
2 teaspoons sugar
½ teaspoon white pepper
1 teaspoon sesame oil

OTHER INGREDIENTS
½ cup fresh ginger, cut into matchstick-sized pieces
2 whole green onions, white part mashed, green cut into 1-inch pieces
2 tablespoons vegetable oil

Thoroughly clean the fish, removing fins, and head if desired. Lay the fish flat and score it crosswise at 1-inch intervals, on both sides. Cut gashes to about ¼ inch from the bone.

Fill a large wok with enough water to almost reach the bottom of a steamer rack. Bring to a boil. Place heatproof plate on top. Be careful not to allow water to touch the plate. Place fish on plate. Bring the water to a rolling boil.

Combine topping mixture in a small bowl and pour mixture over the fish. Scatter ginger and pieces of green onion on top of the fish. Cover tightly, and cook over medium high heat for 15 to 20 minutes, until the base of the thickest part of fish is white.

When fish is almost cooked, heat 2 tablespoons of vegetable oil in a small pan over low heat. As soon as fish is done, transfer to a serving platter. Scatter the remaining onion over the fish.

Serves 3–4.

Steamed Salmon Steaks

Almost as simple as it gets in cooking steps. The steaming process brings out the natural flavors of the salmon.

1½ pound fresh salmon steaks, cut to ¾-inch thickness
1 whole green onion, cut into 1-inch pieces
2–3 slices fresh ginger, cut into matchstick-sized pieces
2 teaspoons rice wine or dry sherry
3 teaspoons vegetable oil
2 tablespoons minced green onion

Fill a large wok with enough water to almost reach the bottom of a steamer rack. Bring to a boil. Place heatproof plate on top. Be careful not to allow water to touch the plate. Place salmon on plate; sprinkle green onion, ginger, and wine on salmon. Steam over high heat until pale pink on the outside, approximately 6 minutes.

Heat oil and minced green onion in a small pan. Pour on top of the fish right before serving.

Steamed Whole Sand Dab with Brown Sauce

2 whole sand dabs, approximately 2 pounds total

TOPPING FOR FISH
1 heaping tablespoon brown bean sauce (min see sauce)
1 tablespoon soy sauce
2 teaspoons rice wine or dry sherry
1 teaspoon oyster sauce
½ teaspoon salt
dash of sugar
dash of white pepper
½ teaspoon sesame oil

OTHER INGREDIENTS
2 slices of fresh ginger, approximately 1 by 1½ inches, cut into thin pieces
2 tablespoons vegetable oil
1 green onion, white part mashed, green part cut into 1-inch pieces

Thoroughly clean the fish, removing head if desired. Lay the fish flat and cut into halves or three parts on the steaming plate.

Fill a large wok with enough water to almost reach the bottom of a steamer rack. Bring to a boil. Place heatproof plate on steamer rack. Be careful not to allow water to touch the plate. Place brown bean sauce in a bowl and gently mash with end of cleaver. Combine with remainder the topping mixture and pour over the fish. Scatter ginger and green onion pieces on fish. Place the fish on the steamer plate, cover tightly, and cook over medium high heat for about 10–12 minutes, until the base of the thickest part of fish turns white.

When the fish is almost cooked, heat 2 tablespoons of vegetable oil in a small pan over low heat. As soon as the fish is done, transfer to a serving platter. Scatter the remaining green onion over the fish; drizzle the hot oil on top.

Serves 2–3.

Stir-Fried Bittermelon with Prawns

Bittermelon is an acquired taste. It is a vegetable that you eat because "it's good for you" when you are a kid, but which you may eat when you are older because you know it IS good for you. Mother now tells me that science confirms what she knew all along: one reason bittermelon is "good for you" is because it contains quinine, the remedy for malaria.

1 pound fresh bittermelon
⅔ pound medium or tiger
   prawns, shelled, deveined,
   rinsed, and patted dry

BLACK BEAN SAUCE
SEE RECIPE *Master Black Bean
   Sauce*, PAGE 201

OTHER INGREDIENTS
1 tablespoon vegetable oil
1 yellow onion, thinly sliced
1 teaspoon sugar
1 cup chicken broth
1 tablespoon cornstarch
   mixed well with 2 tablespoons cold water
hot chili oil or dash of white
   pepper to taste (optional)

Rinse bittermelon, cut in half lengthwise, and remove seeds. Cut into thin (½-inch) slices. Blanch in boiling water or chicken broth for 1 minute and drain well.

Heat wok with oil, swirling to coat sides. Stir-fry onion and bittermelon for 1 minute, over medium heat, until onion turns translucent. Add prawns and black bean sauce and stir-fry for 3 minutes over high heat until prawns turn pink and are cooked. Add sugar and mix for 1 minute. Add broth, bring to a boil, and gently stir in cornstarch mixture and cook an additional minute. Serve immediately.

Serves 2–3.

Poultry

Bittermelon with Chicken in Black Bean Sauce

Beggar's Chicken

Cantonese Curry Chicken

Cashew Chicken with Snow Peas

Chicken and Shrimp Fried Rice

Chicken Rice Pot

Chicken with Baby Bok Choy

Chicken with Black Bean Sauce

Chicken with Long Beans

Chinese Chicken Salad—Sow See Gai

Claypot Chicken

Claypot Lemon Chicken

Crispy Lemon Chicken

Drunken Chicken

Drunken Chicken II

Garlic Chicken with Broccoli

Kung Pao Chicken

Lemon Grass and Basil Chicken

Mu Shu Chicken

Paper-Wrapped Chicken

Steamed Chicken with Black Mushrooms

Steamed Chicken with Ginseng and Black Mushrooms

Steamed Chicken with Tangerine Peel

Steamed Whole Chicken

Stir-fried Chicken with Spinach

Sweet and Sour Chicken Gold Nuggets

Warm Chicken and Noodle Salad

chicken in every pot" was President Herbert Hoover's campaign slogan in 1928, and my Wok Wiz slogan is "a chicken in every wok." Why not? Chicken is popular with diners of all ages, and is prepared Chinese-style in every conceivable way: stir-fried, steamed, deep-fried, poached, stewed, braised, simmered, and smoked. This versatile low-fat meat provides an excellent source of protein at a very reasonable price.

Chicken skin contains much of the fat in chicken, so those who are watching their fat and calorie intake will want to remove the skin. Many of the Chinese recipes here call for removal of the skin. But don't throw the skin away. The carcass and skin of a boned chicken make an excellent base for homemade chicken broth. My philosophy of life is that you can't be too rich, too thin, or have too much chicken broth. Along with chicken skin and carcass, add the following to a stock pot for an aromatic and flavorful broth, to use for soup or cooking: the discarded peel from ginger root, the tips from green onion, core of a cabbage—whatever vegetables you are cooking. For best results, refrigerate the broth, and before using, skim off the fat that forms on top.

Although it's not my personal choice at a dim sum luncheon, many people love braised chicken feet. Others buy it primarily to add flavor to soups. In Hong Kong, four times more chicken feet are sold than chickens, so chicken feet are imported from Canada and elsewhere to meet consumer demand.

Chicken is prepared whole (steamed, stuffed, roasted), or cut up into parts for various dishes. Chicken breast and thigh meat are used primarily for stir-fry cooking. On festive occasions, the chicken is served whole, with the head intact. A simply steamed or roasted chicken is a must at Chinese banquets, because the word for chicken sounds like the word for wealth.

Since salmonella is a common bacterial infection in chickens, it is important to handle it properly. After boning or cutting a chicken, the cutting boards, knives and utensils must be washed thoroughly with soap and water, and wiped completely dry. I usually cut up other ingredients like ginger, garlic, onion and other vegetables before I work with the chicken, or use a second cutting board. After the chicken is cut and perhaps marinated, if it isn't cooked right away, it should be covered and refrigerated.

Bittermelon with Chicken in Black Bean Sauce

Like most children, I didn't find bittermelon to be tasty. My parents cooked it regularly because it was good for us, so naturally it was not meant to be delicious. To cut the bitterness, some cooks like to blanch it in a small amount of water with salt.

1 pound boned chicken thighs, skin removed

MARINADE FOR CHICKEN
2 teaspoons soy sauce
2 teaspoons dry sherry or rice wine
dash of cornstarch
¼ teaspoon white pepper

OTHER INGREDIENTS
3 medium Chinese dried black mushrooms
1 pound fresh bittermelon
1 yellow onion, thinly sliced

BLACK BEAN SAUCE
1 heaping tablespoon fermented black beans
2 teaspoons minced garlic
½ teaspoon sugar
1 teaspoon soy sauce
1 teaspoon dry sherry or rice wine

OTHER INGREDIENTS
1 teaspoon sugar
1 tablespoon vegetable oil
1 cup chicken broth
1 tablespoon cornstarch mixed well with 2 tablespoons liquid reserved from soaking mushrooms

Prepare marinade mixture by blending soy sauce, wine, cornstarch and white pepper. Cover chicken thighs with mixture and marinate for 30 minutes.

Soak mushrooms in hot water for 10 minutes. Squeeze out excess water, reserving liquid to add to cornstarch mixture. Remove and discard stems, and cut caps into thirds. Rinse bittermelon. Cut in half lengthwise, remove seeds, and then cut into ½-inch slices. Blanch bittermelon in a pot of boiling water for 1 minute, remove and drain well.

PREPARE THE BLACK BEAN SAUCE: place black beans and garlic in a small bowl and mash with the end of a cleaver. Stir in sugar, soy sauce and wine.

Heat wok with oil, swirling to coat sides. Stir-fry chicken over high heat for 2–3 minutes until it turns white. Remove chicken and set aside. Reheat wok, adding a touch more oil only if wok appears dry. Stir-fry onion, mushrooms, and bittermelon for 2 minutes.

Return chicken to wok, add black bean sauce and mix well for an additional 2 minutes. Add sugar and broth, bring to a boil, and gently stir in cornstarch mixture and allow to cook another minute until sauce thickens slightly.

Serves 3–4.

Beggar's Chicken

According to legend, Beggar's Chicken was created when a beggar once stole a chicken from a farm. Since he did not have access to a kitchen, he encased the chicken in mud, and tossed it into an open fire. After it was cooked, the clay and feathers of the chicken came off easily, and the beggar had a feast. We thank Julian Mao for his adaptation of Beggar's Chicken recipe for the modern kitchen. Beggar's Chicken is the Mandarin Restaurant's signature dish.

3-pound fryer chicken
1 tablespoon rice wine or sherry
1 heaping teaspoon salt
1 teaspoon sesame oil
¼ teaspoon five-spice powder
1 tablespoon soy sauce
1 pound ceramic clay (obtainable in most art supply shops)

STUFFING FOR CHICKEN
Slice the following into uniform 1-inch long and ¼-inch wide pieces:
  ¼ cup Virginia ham
  ¼ cup bamboo shoots
  ¼ cup waterchestnuts
  ¼ cup Chinese dried black mushrooms

Soak mushrooms in hot water for 10 minutes. Drain excess water, remove and discard stems. Wash and dry the chicken thoroughly. Do not cut the skin of the chicken anywhere, other than cutting off the tailpiece, trimming off the tips of the wings and the neck opening. Combine the rice wine, salt, sesame oil, five-spice powder and soy sauce, and rub the entire bird inside and out with the mixture, reserving the residue to add to the stuffing. After stuffing the bird, do not sew it up but re-form it into its natural shape by cradling it in your hands.

Wrap the bird in a piece of aluminum foil large enough to envelope it completely. Then insert the chicken into a brown paper bag. Next mix the ceramic clay to a stiff paste by adding cold water to it gradually, making sure that it is not too watery and is thoroughly mixed. Use a spatula to apply the entire mixture all over the paper bag evenly and smoothly to make a casing about ¼-inch thick.

Preheat the oven for 10 minutes at 550 degrees, put in the chicken and reduce heat to 475 degrees. Bake for one hour and 45 minutes. Reduce heat to 300 degrees, and bake for 30 minutes.

Remove the bird from the oven and bring it to the table on a metal dish. Cover the clay with a cloth, and strike it sharply with a mallet. Open the bag and foil and serve.

Serves 4-6.

Cantonese Curry Chicken

Use your favorite brand of curry powder. For simplicity, I recommend purchasing curry power in a food market, though it can be made from scratch.

1 whole chicken, 2 ½–3 pounds

MARINADE FOR CHICKEN
1 tablespoon soy sauce
1 tablespoon rice wine
1 teaspoon ginger, minced

OTHER INGREDIENTS
1 tablespoon vegetable oil
1 yellow onion, cut into 1-inch chunks
6 cloves garlic, minced
3 tablespoons curry powder
1 cup chicken broth
1 whole green bell pepper, cut to 1-inch square chunks (for additional color use ½ red and ½ green pepper)
1 tablespoon cornstarch mixed with 2 tablespoons cold water
1 tablespoon minced green onion

Cut up chicken Chinese-style, remove as much of the skin as possible. Use a heavy chopper to cut chicken into 2–3-inch pieces with the bone left in. Place chicken pieces in a large bowl and add marinade ingredients. Marinate for 30 minutes.

Heat wok with oil until smoky. Add onion and garlic and stir-fry until onion is translucent. Drain any excess marinade from chicken and add chicken to wok. Cook over high heat until meat is braised. Turn heat down to medium, and add curry powder and chicken broth. Cover and cook for 45 minutes to an hour, turning occasionally until chicken is tender. Add bell peppers and cook for an additional 4–5 minutes. Stir in cornstarch mixture and cook until sauce thickens slightly. Top with minced green onion.

Serves 4–5.

Cashew Chicken with Snow Peas

This is excellent over rice as a "rice plate." Deep-fried walnut halves may be used instead of cashews. To deep fry walnuts, place them in boiling water for 30 minutes. Drain well, dry, spread on baking pan lined with paper towels. Place in 300–degree preheated oven for 35 minutes. Remove and check to see if nuts are dry. If not, return to oven for another 15 minutes. Heat a wok or frying pan with 1 cup of vegetable oil (to about 375 degrees). Deep-fry the walnuts until golden brown. Remove and place on paper towels to absorb excess oil. This is a lot of work. Stick to cashews . . .

---

1 pound chicken breast, skin and bones removed, cut to bite-sized pieces

MARINADE FOR CHICKEN
1 tablespoon soy sauce
2 teaspoons dry sherry or rice wine
1 teaspoon fresh ginger, minced

OTHER INGREDIENTS
½ cup roasted cashew nuts
2 tablespoons vegetable oil
1 yellow onion, thinly sliced
½ cup bamboo shoots, thinly sliced
4–5 Chinese dried black mushrooms
4–5 fresh or canned Chinese waterchestnuts, thinly sliced
2 stalks celery, thinly sliced diagonally
½ cup chicken broth
1 tablespoon soy sauce
¼ pound snow peas, strings removed, rinsed
1 teaspoon cornstarch mixed well with 1 teaspoon cold water
1 teaspoon oyster sauce
1–2 drops of sesame oil
1 or 2 drops of hot chili pepper oil

Place chicken pieces in a large bowl and add marinade ingredients. Marinate for 30 minutes.

While chicken is marinating, soak mushrooms for 10 minutes, remove and discard stems, and slice caps to matchstick-sized pieces. Save ½ cup mushroom soaking water to add to broth later. Place raw cashews on a pan, and toast at 350 degrees, for 10–15 minutes until golden brown.

Heat wok with 1 tablespoon oil, swirling to coat sides. Stir-fry the chicken for 2 minutes and remove to a medium-sized bowl. Reheat the wok with another tablespoon of oil. Stir-fry the onion for 30 seconds. Add mushrooms, waterchestnuts, and celery. Stir-fry for 2–3 minutes. Add liquid from soaked mushrooms, chicken broth, and soy sauce.

Return chicken to wok. Add the snow peas; stir in the cornstarch mixture, and continue to stir-fry for a minute until the snow peas are cooked and sauce thickens. Stir in the toasted cashew nuts. Mix everything together. Add oyster sauce. Transfer to serving platter. Season with sesame oil and chili oil, if desired.

Serves 3–4.

Chicken and Shrimp Fried Rice

4 Chinese dried black
  mushrooms
1 tablespoon vegetable oil
1 egg
1 yellow onion, minced
½ cup cooked chicken meat
  (white or dark leftover meat
  suggested)
½ cup bay (cocktail) shrimp or
  medium-sized prawns,
  peeled, deveined, rinsed,
  and coarsely chopped
2 cups cold cooked rice,
  (refrigerated overnight is best)
1 tablespoon soy sauce
¼ cup fresh or frozen green
  peas
¼ head small iceberg lettuce or
  other favorite lettuce,
  shredded
1 tablespoon minced green
  onion
½ teaspoon white pepper
1 teaspoon sesame oil

Soak mushrooms in hot water for 10 minutes, squeeze out excess water, remove and discard stems, and dice caps into small pieces.

Heat wok with 1 teaspoon oil, swirling to coat sides. Add egg, and cook omelet-style. Remove and set aside.

Reheat wok with remaining oil, swirling to coat sides. Add onion, black mushrooms, chicken, and shrimp. Cook until onion is translucent. Stir in rice and add soy sauce, mixing all ingredients except for eggs together for several minutes over high heat.

Return eggs to wok. Add green peas and toss and everything together for 1 minute, until green peas are cooked. Add lettuce, toss for another 30 seconds. Top with green onion and white pepper, and drizzle with sesame oil.

Serves 3.

Chicken Rice Pot

This is something I grew up with—we call it "Gai Fon—Chicken Rice." I thought I would be tired of it long before I reached my present age, but some dishes never grow old. The combination of the sweetness of the Chinese sausage and the richness of the mushrooms, mixed with the juice of the chicken and other ingredients makes this a crowd pleaser. My busy mother, who raised 5 children, served this to us frequently. Use a 5-quart pot or casserole to provide ample room for the chicken pieces, other ingredients, and rice, and to make it easy to stir and mix together before serving.

2½ cups long-grain rice
2½–3 pound chicken, excess fat and skin removed, cut to 2-inch bite-sized pieces, bone in

MARINADE FOR CHICKEN
2 tablespoons soy sauce
2 teaspoons ginger, minced
1 tablespoon dry sherry or rice wine
1 heaping teaspoon garlic, minced
1 teaspoon sesame oil
1 teaspoon cornstarch
1 tablespoon vegetable oil

OTHER INGREDIENTS
4 Chinese dried black mushrooms
1 yellow onion, thinly sliced
2 links Chinese sausages (lob cheung), cut diagonally into ½-inch pieces
2 green onions cut into 1-inch pieces
1 tablespoon green onion, minced
1 tablespoon oyster sauce
3–4 drops sesame oil

Place chicken in a large bowl and add marinade ingredients. Marinate at least 30 minutes.

Soak mushrooms in hot water 10 minutes, squeeze out excess water, remove and discard stems, and cut caps into thirds.

Place rice in a pot and rinse rice several times to wash out excess starch and prevent cooked rice from being gummy. Pour out the water carefully and repeat until water runs clear. Transfer the rice to a 5-quart pot or casserole.

Pour water in pot to 1 inch above rice level. Cover and place over high heat. When the water boils rapidly, reduce heat to lowest setting.

While the rice is cooking, heat a wok with oil, swirling to coat sides. Stir-fry the onion, chicken, mushrooms, sausages, and green onions for 3–4 minutes. When the water from the rice pot begins to evaporate, pour the chicken mixture on top. Cover and cook over low heat for 20–25 minutes. Stir in oyster sauce and sesame oil, and top with remaining minced green onions.

Serves 4–6.

Chicken with Baby Bok Choy

Baby bok choy is simple to prepare, is tender in flavor, and attractive to present. Choose baby bok choy that is under 6 inches long for the best results. Chinese vegetables are often grown in sandy soil, so rinse well in cold water. Always trim the bottom inch or so before rinsing.

1 chicken breast or 2 thighs, boned, skin removed, and cut into bite-sized pieces

MARINADE FOR CHICKEN
1 teaspoon fresh ginger, minced
1 large clove garlic, minced
1 tablespoon soy sauce
1 tablespoon dry sherry or rice wine
1 teaspoon sugar
1 teaspoon cornstarch
½ teaspoon sesame oil

OTHER INGREDIENTS
8 Chinese dried black mushrooms
1 pound baby bok choy
2 cups chicken broth
2 teaspoons vegetable oil
2 green onions, cut to 1-inch pieces
1 piece of fresh ginger, 1 by 2 inches, cut into matchstick-sized pieces
½ cup yellow onion, thinly sliced
1 teaspoon cornstarch mixed well with 2 teaspoons cold water

Mix marinade ingredients in a large bowl and marinate chicken pieces for 30 minutes.

Soak mushrooms in hot water 10 minutes. Squeeze out excess water, remove and discard stems, and cut caps into halves. Cut off bok choy stems, rinse well and keep smaller bok choy in whole pieces. If large, cut vertically into 2–inch lengths.

Pour 2 cups chicken broth into a 3-quart stockpot and bring to a boil. Blanch baby bok choy for one minute. Drain and set aside.

Heat wok with oil, swirling to coat sides. Stir-fry ginger and onion until onion is translucent. With the heat still very high, add the mushrooms and chicken and keep stir-frying, to seal in the marinade and create a coating on the meat. Add 1 cup chicken broth and bring to a boil. Stir in cornstarch mixture and continue cooking until sauce thickens slightly. Add extra soy sauce if desired. Arrange baby bok choy on serving platter, in a fan-like pattern from the center out and place chicken on top of the greens.

Serves 3–4.

Chicken with Black Bean Sauce

¾ pound skinned and boned chicken breast and/or thigh, cut into 1-inch bite-sized pieces

MARINADE FOR CHICKEN
1 tablespoon soy sauce
1 teaspoon rice wine or dry sherry

BLACK BEAN SAUCE
(SEE RECIPE, *Master Black Bean Sauce,* PAGE 201

OTHER INGREDIENTS
1 tablespoon vegetable oil
1 yellow onion, cut into 1-inch chunks
½ medium green bell pepper, cut into 1-inch squares
⅔ cup chicken broth
1 tablespoon cornstarch mixed with 2 tablespoons cold water
½ teaspoon sesame oil
hot chili oil to taste
½ cup green onion, minced

Place chicken in a bowl, add marinade, and marinate for at least 30 minutes.

Prepare black bean sauce and set aside.

Heat wok with oil, swirling to coat sides. When smoky, add yellow onion and cook until translucent. While the wok is still very hot, add chicken and stir-fry quickly until meat begins to turn white. Add black bean sauce and blend well. Add green bell peppers and chicken broth. Bring to a boil. Stir in cornstarch mixture and continue to cook until sauce thickens. Add more soy sauce to suit personal taste. Drizzle with sesame oil, and hot chili oil if desired. Top with minced green onion.

Serves 3–4.

Chicken with Long Beans (Dow Gawk)

If Chinese long beans are not available, use regular string beans or another vegetable, such as asparagus, broccoli or cauliflower. For an attractive presentation, cook long beans separately, place on serving platter, and serve chicken on top.

1 whole chicken breast, skinned, boned, cut to bite-sized pieces
½ pound Chinese long beans, trimmed and cut to 2-inch pieces

MARINADE FOR CHICKEN
1 tablespoon soy sauce
1 tablespoon rice wine or dry sherry
1 teaspoon cornstarch

BLACK BEAN SAUCE
1 heaping tablespoon fermented black beans, rinsed and drained
1 tablespoon garlic, minced
1 teaspoon rice wine or dry sherry
1 tablespoon soy sauce
½ teaspoon sugar

OTHER INGREDIENTS
2 tablespoons vegetable oil
1 yellow onion, thinly sliced
1 tablespoon fresh ginger, minced
½ cup chicken broth
1 teaspoon cornstarch mixed well with 2 teaspoons cold water

Place chicken in a small bowl and toss with soy sauce, sherry, and cornstarch.

Blanch the long beans in 2–3 cups of water or chicken broth for 15–30 seconds. Drain and set aside.

Prepare black bean sauce: place black beans and garlic in a small bowl and mash together with the end of a cleaver. Stir in soy sauce, wine, and sugar.

Heat wok with 1 tablespoon oil, swirling to coat sides. When the oil is smoky, stir-fry the chicken and ginger for about 2 minutes, until meat begins to turn white. Add onion, long beans, and black bean sauce, and stir over high heat. Add broth and bring to a boil. Gradually stir in cornstarch mixture and continue to cook until sauce thickens.

Serves 2–3.

Chinese Chicken Salad (Sow See Gai)

Every Asian chef that I know has a Chinese Chicken Salad. There are so many recipes, someone should write a book on this popular first course. Here is my contribution. Another possibility for a dressing is a ready-made sesame-flavored style. Or use your favorite dressing.

2½ cups vegetable oil
1 half chicken, approximately
   1½ pounds

MARINADE FOR CHICKEN
¼ cup soy sauce
1 teaspoon fresh ginger,
   minced
1 teaspoon garlic, minced
½ cup rice wine or dry sherry

OTHER INGREDIENTS
¼ cup unsalted peanuts
1 tablespoon sesame seeds
2 cups vegetable oil
2 ounces rice sticks (mai fun)
2 green onions, white part
   mashed, green part cut into
   1-inch pieces
1 tablespoon rice vinegar
favorite salad dressing or
   2 teaspoons hot mustard
   powder mixed with 1 tablespoon cold water and ½ cup
   rice vinegar
½ teaspoon sesame oil
½ head finely-shredded
   iceberg lettuce
⅛ teaspoon 5-spice powder
Chinese parsley (cilantro)
   sprigs for garnish

Combine the marinade ingredients in a large bowl and add chicken to marinate for 1–2 hours.

Place the chicken on a rack in a large baking pan and bake for approximately 1 hour at 350 degrees until cooked. After chicken cools, remove and discard the skin and bones and shred the meat by hand or with cleaver. At the same time, roast the peanuts in a 350-degree oven to a golden brown (a toaster oven is very handy), approximately 10 minutes. Allow to cool, then crush the nuts. Toast sesame seeds in a small fry pan over medium heat, shaking gently, until golden brown.

In a large wok heat up oil over high heat. Test oil by placing one small piece of rice stick in hot oil. If it puffs up quickly, the oil is ready. Gradually place small handfuls of rice stick in wok. Drain excess oil on paper towels.

Heat second large wok—do not add oil. Add the chicken, green onions, rice vinegar, and toss well. Turn heat off. Add either the mustard and sesame oil mixture, or favorite prepared sesame oil salad dressing. Add the lettuce and 5-spice. Sprinkle rice sticks (mai fun) over the top of salad and toss again. Sprinkle with crushed nuts and sesame seeds. Top with Chinese parsley. Serve extra rice sticks and salad dressing on the side.

Serves 3–4

Claypot Chicken

This recipe uses an old-time method of stewing in a claypot. It is wondrous how the flavors blend together over low heat. It is excellent for dinner parties, as once all the food is put into the claypot, it can be set on the burner to cook while the rest of the meal is prepared.

8 Chinese dried black mushrooms
1 small head napa cabbage, leaves separated
1/3 cup water
1 fryer chicken (2 1/2–3 pounds), cut in bite-sized pieces, bone in, skin removed if desired
2 tablespoons soy sauce
2 cloves garlic, minced
2 slices fresh ginger, 1 by 2 inches, cut to matchstick-sized pieces
1/4 teaspoon sugar
2 tablespoons rice wine or dry sherry
2 whole star anise, broken into small pieces
1 teaspoon cornstarch
2 tablespoons vegetable oil
1 cup chicken broth
2 teaspoons cornstarch mixed well with 1 tablespoon cold water and 1 teaspoon soy sauce
1 green onion, cut to 1-inch pieces
1 teapoon sesame oil
Chinese parsley (cilantro)
1 teaspoon hot-chili sesame oil

Soak mushrooms in hot water for 10 minutes. Squeeze out excess water, remove and discard stems, and leave caps whole. Line a 2-quart claypot with napa cabbage leaves. Add water and set aside. Place chicken pieces in a bowl and add soy sauce, garlic, ginger, mushrooms, sugar, wine, and star anise. Blend all the ingredients and stir together. Add one teaspoon cornstarch and mix well.

Place wok over high heat until hot. Add vegetable oil, swirling to coat sides. Brown chicken pieces on all sides. Transfer chicken to the claypot lined with cabbage leaves. Add chicken broth. Place claypot on range top and gradually bring to a boil, stirring gently. Cover and simmer over low heat for 45 minutes to an hour, until chicken is cooked and tender. Stir in cornstarch mixture and continue to cook until sauce thickens slightly. Top with green onion and drizzle with sesame oil. Bring claypot to table to serve. For some spiciness, drizzle in 1 teaspoon of hot-chili-sesame oil. Garnish with a generous handful of fresh, chopped Chinese parsley.

Serves 4–6.

Claypot Lemon Chicken

When my husband Bernie Carver was a student in my Chinese cooking class, this was his favorite dish. For health reasons, he prefers this version of Lemon Chicken to the one which requires the chicken to be deep-fried. Skin is also removed to further reduce fat content.

---

1 chicken, approximately 2½ pounds, cut to bite-sized pieces, bone in, skin removed if desired
1 head napa cabbage, leaves separated
⅓ cup water
2 cloves garlic, minced
2 slices fresh ginger, 1 by 2 inches, cut to matchstick-sized pieces
½ teaspoon sugar
3–4 tablespoons rice wine or dry sherry
3 tablespoons soy sauce
2 whole star anise
2 dried chili peppers, broken into halves

LEMON SAUCE
⅓ cup lemon juice
⅓ cup packed brown sugar

OTHER INGREDIENTS
2 tablespoons vegetable oil
1 cup chicken broth
1 tablespoon cornstarch mixed well with 2 tablespoons cold water
1 green onion, cut in 1-inch pieces

Remove excess fat and cut chicken into serving pieces, bone-in. Skin may also be removed.

Line claypot with cabbage leaves. Add ⅓ cup cold water and set aside. Blend garlic, ginger, sugar, wine, soy sauce, star anise, and chili peppers in a small bowl.

Prepare lemon sauce by combining lemon juice and brown sugar until sugar dissolves. Add ½ of the cornstarch mixture and continue cooking until sauce thickens slightly. Remove from heat.

Place wok over high heat until hot. Add vegetable oil, swirling to coat sides. When the oil is hot, brown chicken pieces on all sides.

Transfer chicken to the claypot lined with cabbage leaves. Add blended mixture of garlic, ginger, soy sauce, wine, anise, chili pepper and chicken broth to pot and mix well. Place claypot on range top, and raise heat gradually to a boil, stirring gently. Cover and simmer over low heat for 45 minutes to 1 hour, until chicken is cooked. Add cornstarch mixture and continue to cook until sauce thickens slightly. Stir in lemon sauce. Adjust sauce if necessary. Garnish with green onions. Bring claypot to the table to serve.

Serves 4–6.

Crispy Lemon Chicken

2 chicken breast halves
⅛ teaspoon white pepper
1 tablespoon rice wine or dry
 sherry

LEMON SAUCE
8 ounces crushed pineapple
 (or one small can), reserve
 juice
¼ cup fresh lemon juice
3 tablespoons packed brown
 sugar
1 tablespoon rice or white
 vinegar
1 tablespoon cornstarch

DEEP-FRYING BATTER
1 cup cornstarch
1 cup all-purpose flour or ½
 cup prepared baking mix and
 ½ cup all-purpose flour
1 cup water
1 egg
1 teaspoon baking powder
1 teaspoon oil

OTHER INGREDIENTS
3 cups vegetable oil
thin slices of lemon
Chinese parsley (cilantro) for
 garnish

Split and bone chicken breasts. Carefully slice each chicken breast horizontally into two even halves, trimming excess fat from skin. Place in a shallow bowl and sprinkle with white pepper and wine.

In a medium saucepan, place lemon sauce ingredients over medium-high heat. Be careful not to let the sauce boil. Set aside. In a bowl, mix together the batter ingredients to pancake-batter consistency. Refrigerate 10 minutes to set.

Heat a wok, electric wok, or frying pan with vegetable oil for deep-frying, approximately 350–375 degrees. Dip chicken into prepared batter. Carefully deep-fry each breast for 4–5 minutes until golden brown. Cut chicken into strips and arrange on a platter. Pour lemon sauce over chicken. Garnish with lemon slices around the platter and top with parsley.

Serves: 3–4.

Drunken Chicken

I have had many friends and cooking students ask about this recipe—they wonder how I got the chicken to drink, what the chicken's problems were, and whether the chicken has to enter a recovery program.

1 whole chicken, 3–3½
    pounds, excess fat removed,
    rinsed well and patted dry
4 quarts water
1 heaping teaspoon fresh
    ginger, mashed and coarsely
    chopped

MARINADE FOR CHICKEN
1 cup light rum or rice wine
⅓ cup chicken broth
1 heaping teaspoon fresh
    ginger, minced
2 tablespoons soy sauce
1 tablespoon sugar
½ teaspoon white pepper
Chinese parsley (cilantro) or a
    sprinkling of minced green
    onion for garnish

Fill a large pot with 4 quarts of water and bring to a near-boil. Add mashed ginger and cook for 1 minute. Add chicken and more hot water if necessary to cover entire chicken. Reduce heat, cover and simmer for 45 minutes to an hour, until chicken is cooked (test by checking meat of a thigh bone—if it's no longer pink, the chicken is done). Remove chicken and cool completely. Remove skin and bones. Shred or cut into bite-sized pieces. Place in a large bowl and add marinade ingredients. Cover with plastic wrap. Refrigerate for several hours or overnight. Garnish with Chinese parsley or minced green onion, and serve cold as a salad or side dish.

Serves 3–4.

Drunken Chicken II (with Papaya and Cognac)

I developed this recipe on the spot as a guest chef/demonstrator for a fund-raiser in San Francisco's Chinatown. I returned from Hawaii two days prior to the show, ready to create a tropically inspired dish. I was introduced to macadamia nut oil during my visit to Oahu, and Martell VSOP Cognac was one of the sponsors for the event to benefit Self-Help for the Elderly, so I used both the nut oil and cognac. Nutrition-conscious cooks will be pleased to learn that half a papaya provides nearly twice an adult's recommended daily amount of Vitamin C, while containing only about 80 calories.

1 pound boneless chicken breast, cut into bite-sized pieces

MARINADE FOR CHICKEN
3 tablespoons soy sauce
1 tablespoon dry sherry, rice wine, or cognac
1 teaspoon cornstarch

OTHER INGREDIENTS
6 Chinese dried black mushrooms
2 tablespoons macadamia nut oil or other vegetable oil
1 yellow onion, thinly sliced
1 heaping teaspoon fresh ginger, minced
6–8 straw mushrooms (usually found in cans) (optional)
1 cup Chinese yellow chives, cut into 2–inch pieces
¾ cup chicken broth
1 tablespoon cornstarch mixed well with 2 tablespoons cold water
1 firm papaya, cut into 1-inch cubes
½ cup cognac—Martell VSOP or other quality brand cognac
Chinese parsley (cilantro) sprigs

Combine the marinade ingredients. Cover chicken with mixture, and marinate for 30 minutes. Cognac should be at room temperature before using.

Soak mushrooms in hot water for 10 minutes, squeeze out excess water, remove and discard stems, and leave caps whole.

Heat wok with 1 tablespoon oil, swirling to coat sides. Stir-fry black mushrooms, onion, ginger, straw mushrooms, and yellow chives until onion is translucent. Remove to a platter.

Reheat wok with remaining oil. Stir-fry chicken for 2–3 minutes over high heat, until meat changes color and is braised. Return other ingredients to wok. Add chicken broth and bring to a boil. Stir in cornstarch mixture to form a light gravy. Add papaya and blend with other ingredients. Cook for 1 minute. Immediately before serving, stir in the ½ cup cognac. Top with sprigs of Chinese parsley.

Serves 2–3.

Garlic Chicken with Broccoli

Garlic lovers will increase the amount of garlic here to suit personal taste. This is another simple, yet tasty recipe.

1 whole chicken breast, skinned, boned, cut to bite-sized pieces

MARINADE FOR CHICKEN
2 tablespoons soy sauce
1 teaspoon fresh ginger, minced
½ teaspoon sesame oil
1 tablespoon rice wine or dry sherry

OTHER INGREDIENTS
2 tablespoons vegetable oil
1 yellow onion, thinly sliced
8 cloves garlic, minced
1 cup chicken broth
2 teaspoons cornstarch mixed with 1 tablespoon cold water
1 pound broccoli; keep small florets whole, cut larger florets lengthwise into halves or quarters; stems trimmed diagonally into 1-inch pieces
1 teaspoon soy sauce

Mix marinade ingredients and marinate chicken for at least 30 minutes.

Heat wok with 1 tablespoon vegetable oil, swirling to coat sides. Stir-fry the onion, garlic and chicken, for 3–4 minutes until onion becomes translucent, garlic turns golden, and chicken browns and is cooked through.

Add ½ cup of chicken broth, bring to a boil and mix in half of the cornstarch mixture. Continue to cook until sauce thickens slightly. Remove from wok and keep warm. Add remaining tablespoon of oil to clean wok, swirling to coat sides. Add broccoli and cook quickly over high heat. Add remaining ½ cup of chicken broth and soy sauce, and cook for 2–3 minutes until broccoli turns bright green and most of the broth evaporates. Stir in remaining cornstarch mixture. Place broccoli on serving platter and top with garlic chicken.

Serves 2–3.

Kung Pao Chicken

This dish is a favorite of most people who like spicy food. Adjust the spiciness by adding more peppers or chili oil.

1 whole chicken breast, skinned, boned, and cut to bite-sized pieces

MARINADE FOR CHICKEN
1 tablespoon soy sauce
2 teaspoons rice wine or dry sherry
1 teaspoon fresh ginger, minced
¼ teaspoon sesame oil
1 teaspoon hot chili oil

OTHER INGREDIENTS
1 tablespoon vegetable oil
1 teaspoon hot chili pepper oil
2 or 3 whole chili peppers (optional)
1 yellow onion, sliced
1 bell pepper, diced into ½-inch pieces
7 ounces of firm tofu, diced into ½-inch cubes
1 cup chicken broth
1 tablespoon hoisin sauce
1 tablespoon oyster sauce
2 tablespoons rice wine or dry sherry
1 tablespoon cornstarch mixed with 2 tablespoons cold water
½ cup roasted peanuts

Combine the marinade ingredients in a large bowl and toss with the chicken. Marinate for 2–3 hours.

Heat wok with 1 tablespoon vegetable and 1 teaspoon chili pepper oil, swirling to coat sides. Stir-fry the whole chili peppers for a few seconds. When they turn black, remove and discard.

Add onion and chicken and stir-fry over high heat to sear the meat. Add bell pepper, and continue to stir-fry for 2 minutes. Gently fold in tofu and chicken broth. Blend in hoisin sauce, oyster sauce, and wine, and bring to a near boil. Add the cornstarch mixture and continue to cook until sauce thickens slightly. Sprinkle in roasted peanuts.

Serves 2–3.

Lemon Grass and Basil Chicken

This is a diversion of sorts from Chinese cooking, using traditionally southeast Asian ingredients of lemon grass and basil. It seems, however, a melting pot within a melting pot is emerging in the food scene.

1 whole chicken breast, boneless and skinless, cut into bite-sized pieces

MARINADE FOR CHICKEN
1 tablespoon fresh lemon grass (peel tough outer layers, crush and use the bulb-like base only)
1 tablespoon fish sauce (nam pla)
1 teaspoon rice or white vinegar
1 teaspoon sugar
1 teaspoon cornstarch
1 teaspoon white pepper

OTHER INGREDIENTS
1 tablespoon vegetable oil
3 cloves garlic, minced
½ teaspoon fresh ginger, minced
½ yellow onion, thinly sliced
3 whole chili peppers
¼ cup fresh basil leaves
½ cup chicken broth
1 teaspoon cornstarch mixed well with 2 teaspoons cold water
½ teaspoon hot chili pepper oil
sesame oil to taste
extra basil leaves for garnish

Combine marinade ingredients in a large bowl. Marinate chicken for at least 1 hour, longer preferred.

Heat wok with oil. When smoky, add garlic, ginger, onion, and chili peppers. Cook until onion is translucent.

Add chicken and continue to stir-fry over high heat.

Add basil leaves, cook for a minute, and add chicken broth. Bring to a boil and stir in cornstarch mixture until sauce thickens. Drizzle with small amounts of hot chili pepper oil and sesame oil. Top with basil leaves.

Serves 2–3.

Mu Shu Chicken

Cholesterol counters can pan-fry egg into a crepe, cut into matchstick-sized pieces and serve separately on a plate alongside the green onions and hoisin sauce. Guests choose to add the egg or leave it out. If there is leftover filling, spread a small amount of hoisin sauce on leaves of iceberg or other favorite lettuce, fill with leftover from mu shu chicken, and eat as a taco!

---

12 pancakes (RECIPE ON PAGE
   179) or 1 package mu shu
   pork wrappers (Menlo brand
   is recommended)
¼ cup cloud ear fungus
4 Chinese dried black
   mushrooms
½ chicken breast
1 tablespoon rice wine or dry
   sherry
1 tablespoon soy sauce
1 teaspoon cornstarch
2 tablespoons vegetable oil
3 eggs, lightly beaten
1 cup spinach, finely
   chopped
½ cup green onions, finely
   minced
¼ cup shredded bamboo
   shoots
1 teaspoon soy sauce
1 teaspoon sesame oil
½ cup hoisin sauce
½ cup green onion, cut into
   thin slivers

Soak mushrooms in hot water for 10 minutes, squeeze out excess water, remove and discard stems, and cut caps into thin slivers. Shred the cloud ear fungus.

Slice chicken into thin slivers. Place in a small bowl with wine, soy sauce, and cornstarch. Marinate for 10–15 minutes.

Heat wok. Add 1 tablespoon oil, swirling to coat sides. Stir in eggs and fry omelet-style until golden. Transfer to plate.

Reheat wok with remaining oil. Add the chicken, spinach, green onions, bamboo shoots, soy sauce, and sesame oil. Stir vigorously and cook for 2–3 minutes. Return the eggs to the wok, breaking them up into small pieces. If desired, season with a little more sesame oil. Transfer to a serving platter.

Place some hoisin sauce on a small plate and shredded green onions on another plate. Open a pancake wrapper. Spread the center lightly with hoisin sauce and a few slivers of green onion. Spoon 2 table-spoons of cooked filling into the center of the pancake. Tuck in the bottom end, then roll the wrapper to close over the filling.

Serves 8–10.

Paper–Wrapped Chicken

Instead of oiling the baking dish, use non-stick spray. If there are leftovers, deep-fry them in 2 cups of hot oil for 1 minute, or microwave for 20 seconds at high to heat through. Re-baking will dry out the chicken.

1 whole chicken, approximately 2½ pounds, skin and bones removed and cut to 1- by 2-inch pieces (for simplicity, use chicken breast)

MARINADE FOR CHICKEN
2 tablespoons hoisin sauce
2 teaspoons tomato catsup
2 teaspoons brown or white sugar
2 minced green onions
1 tablespoon soy sauce
1 teaspoon sesame oil
2 tablespoons rice wine or dry sherry

OTHER INGREDIENTS
1 teaspoon cornstarch
waxed paper
1 teaspoon vegetable oil

Place chicken in a medium-sized bowl. Cover with marinade mixture and marinate for at least 1 hour. Meanwhile, cut 15 pieces of 5-inch length waxed paper. Cut each piece in half to make a total of 30 sheets. Place a piece of chicken and dab some marinade in the center of each waxed paper sheet. Fold in half to form a triangle. Fold side edges towards the center, and tuck in remaining corner to form an envelope.

Oil a baking dish lightly. Arrange chicken packets in the dish so they don't touch. Bake at 350 degrees for 6 minutes. Flip and cook the chicken for another 4–5 minutes.

Makes 30.

Steamed Chicken with Black Mushrooms

1 whole chicken breast and 2
chicken legs

MARINADE FOR CHICKEN
1 tablespoon soy sauce
1 tablespoon oyster sauce
1 tablespoon rice wine or dry
sherry
1 teaspoon sugar
1 teaspoon white sugar
1 tablespoon cornstarch or
tapioca powder
¼ teaspoon salt

OTHER INGREDIENTS
8 Chinese dried black
mushrooms
3 Chinese red dates
¼ cup fresh ginger, sliced into
matchstick-sized pieces
1 whole green onion, (mash
white part slightly with side
of cleaver, cut green parts
into 1-inch segments)
2 links of Chinese sausages,
lean type preferred, sliced
diagonally into ¼-inch pieces
3 Chinese waterchestnuts, cut
into thin slices (fresh
preferred)

Remove excess fat from chicken. Use a
meat chopper to chop through bones of
chicken, cutting into bite-sized pieces.
Remove skin if desired. Place chicken in
a large bowl.

In a small bowl, combine all marinade
ingredients and mix well. Add to chicken
and marinate for 30 or more minutes—
the longer, the better.

Soak mushrooms in hot water for 10
minutes. Drain, remove and discard
stems, and leave caps whole. Soak dates
in hot water until soft. Remove pits and
cut into small pieces.

Fill a large wok with enough water to
almost reach steamer rack. Bring the
water to a boil. Place chicken on a
heatproof platter and spread date pieces,
ginger, sausage, and waterchestnut slices
attractively on chicken. Place platter on
steamer rack, cover and steam for 30–35
minutes, until chicken meat turns white.
Remove and serve directly from platter.

Serves 4.

Steamed Chicken with Ginseng and Black Mushrooms

2 large chicken legs
4 Chinese dried black
  mushrooms
½ ounce of good-quality
  ginseng root
1 piece fresh ginger, approximately 1 by 2 inches, cut into
  matchstick-sized pieces
½ cup rice wine or dry sherry
½ cup chicken broth
1 teaspoon cornstarch or
  tapioca starch
dash of white pepper
½ cup finely minced green
  onion

Cut each chicken leg in half at the joint and then in half again. Leave the bone in, but remove skin, rinse well, and pat dry.

Soak mushrooms in hot water for 10 minutes. Squeeze out excess water, remove stems, and cut caps into thirds. Reserve soaking water to add to chicken broth. Soak the ginseng root in hot water until soft. Slice into thin pieces and add soaking water to chicken broth. Place chicken legs on heatproof glass or ceramic deep plate. Top with mush-rooms, ginger, ginseng, and mixture of wine, chicken broth, and cornstarch.

Fill a large wok with enough water to almost reach a steamer rack. Place steaming plate on rack. Bring water to a boil, being careful not to let the water touch the steaming plate. Steam over high heat for 30–35 minutes until chicken is cooked. Before serving, sprinkle with white pepper and minced green onion.

Serves 3–4.

Steamed Chicken with Tangerine Peel

This is a version of my parents' many steamed chicken entrées. The combination of sweet dates, the aromatic citrus scent of the tangerine peel, spiciness of the ginger, and earthy richness of mushrooms gives a complex character to a simple-to-prepare one dish meal.

2 boned chicken thighs plus
  ½ chicken breast
2 pieces dried tangerine peel,
  approximately 1-inch square
4 Chinese red dates
4 Chinese dried black mushrooms
½ cup fresh or canned bamboo shoots, sliced to ⅛-inch
  thin strips
3 pieces fresh ginger, sliced to
  ⅛-inch strips
1 teaspoon sugar
2 tablespoons soy sauce
1 teaspoon cornstarch
1 teaspoon green onion,
  minced
1 teaspoon fresh ginger,
  minced
dash of white pepper

Remove excess fat from chicken and cut into bite-sized pieces. Remove skin if desired. Rinse and towel-dry. Place on steamer plate.

Soak tangerine peel in warm water or until soft and cut into small pieces. Soak dates in warm water for 10–25 minutes. Remove pits and slice into small wedges. Soak mushrooms in hot water for 10 minutes. Squeeze out excess water, remove and discard stems, and cut into thirds.

Place chicken on heatproof steamer plate large enough to hold chicken. Mix chicken, tangerine peel, dates, bamboo shoots, ginger, and mushrooms together in a bowl. Add sugar and soy sauce, and sprinkle of cornstarch. Pour over chicken on steamer plate. Top with green onion and additional ginger.

Fill a large wok with enough water to almost reach the steamer rack. Bring to a boil. Place steamer plate on rack and steam over medium high heat for 30–40 minutes or until chicken cooks. Sprinkle with dash of white pepper.

Serves 3–4.

Steamed Whole Chicken

This goes quite well with ginger, soy sauce and green onion dipping sauce.

12 cups water
1 whole chicken, approximately 3 pounds, excess fat removed
3 slices of fresh ginger root (2 by 2 inches)
2 green onions, cut into 2-inch lengths
1 tablespoon salt
1 tablespoon sugar
1 tablespoon sesame oil

Fill a large pot with water. Add ginger, green onions, salt and sugar. Bring to boil, place chicken in the pot, and cover. Lower heat and simmer for 20 minutes. Flip the chicken, cover again, and simmer for another 20 minutes. Remove from heat, allow chicken to sit in pot for an additional 40 minutes. Drain well, cool until it is easy to handle. Rub chicken with sesame oil, and carve into bite-size pieces. Serve at room temperature or cold.

Serves 5–6.

Stir-Fried Chicken with Spinach

1 whole chicken breast, skin and bones removed, cut into bite-sized pieces

MARINADE FOR CHICKEN
1 tablespoon soy sauce
1 tablespoon rice wine or dry sherry
1 teaspoon cornstarch

OTHER INGREDIENTS
1 teaspoon vegetable oil
3 Chinese dried black mushrooms
1 tablespoon vegetable oil
6 cloves garlic, minced
2 bunches fresh spinach
½ cup chicken broth
1 teaspoon soy sauce
1 teaspoon cornstarch mixed well with 2 teaspoons cold water

Mix chicken with marinade ingredients in a bowl. Marinate for at least 30 minutes.

Soak mushrooms in hot water for 10 minutes. Squeeze out excess water, remove and discard stems, and slice caps into thin pieces.

Heat a wok with oil, swirling to coat sides. Add garlic and mushrooms, and stir-fry until garlic turns golden. Add spinach and cook for 1 minute. Add half of the chicken broth and cook spinach until it turns bright green. Remove spinach and keep warm.

Reheat wok with remaining oil, swirling to coat sides. Add the chicken and cook over high heat, until chicken turns white. Add remaining chicken broth and bring to a boil. Add soy sauce, and cornstarch mixture, and continue to cook until sauce thickens slightly. Place spinach on serving platter and scoop chicken on top.

Serves 2–3.

Sweet and Sour Chicken Gold Nuggets

1 whole chicken breast, skinned, boned, cut into 1-inch cubes
1 tablespoon soy sauce
1 egg white
½ cup flour
½ cup cornstarch
2 cups vegetable oil for deep-frying
½ cup sesame seeds
1 teaspoon oil
½ yellow onion, thinly sliced
1 stalk celery, sliced diagonally into thin pieces

SWEET AND SOUR SAUCE
pineapple juice from 7-ounce can of pineapple chunks
½ cup tomato catsup
3 tablespoons brown sugar
1 cup water
3 tablespoons rice or white vinegar
2 tomatoes, cut into quarters
7 ounces pineapple chunks (one small can)
1 tablespoon cornstarch mixed well with 2 tablespoons cold water

Sprinkle chicken with soy sauce and dip into egg white. Place cornstarch and flour mixture in bowl. Coat a few nuggets of chicken at a time. Shake excess flour off each piece.

Deep-fry chicken, a few nuggets at a time, in hot oil for 2–3 minutes until golden brown. Remove chicken, drain, and set aside. In a small fry pan, roast the sesame seeds, using no oil, until seeds are golden. To a clean wok, add 1 teaspoon oil. Stir-fry onion and celery until onion turns translucent.

To make the sweet and sour sauce combine pineapple juice, catsup, brown sugar, and water in a saucepan over medium heat. Add vinegar, and reduce heat. Add tomatoes and pineapple chunks and mix to blend. Return onion and celery to wok. Stir in cornstarch mixture and continue to cook until sauce thickens slightly, adjusting thickness to taste. Return chicken to wok and toss to mix well with sauce. Top with toasted sesame seeds.

Serves 2–3.

Warm Chicken and Noodle Salad

Try this out as an alternative to chicken salad with the traditional deep-fried rice sticks. Serve as a first course or entrée for lunch or casual parties.

½ cup roasted peanuts or walnuts

1 pound fresh Chinese egg noodles

1 tablespoon vegetable oil

3 cloves garlic, minced

½ green bell pepper, cut into thin strips

½ red bell pepper, cut into thin strips

2 whole boneless chicken breasts, sliced into 1-inch pieces

12 fresh Chinese snow peas, whole, strings removed; if longer than 4 inches, cut in halves (or use 1 cup fresh or frozen green peas)

½ cup green onion, cut into 1-inch pieces

DRESSING FOR SALAD

¼ cup soy sauce

2 tablespoons rice or white vinegar

1 teaspoon hot chili oil

¼ teaspoon crushed red pepper

¼ teaspoon white pepper

Chinese parsley (cilantro)

To roast nuts, place uncooked peanuts or walnuts in oven or on toaster oven tray. Heat oven to 350 degrees. Roast the nuts for 8–10 minutes until golden brown. Transfer from oven tray to plate. When cool, place in blender (or use cleaver) and crush lightly into smaller pieces.

Cook fresh noodles in a large pot of boiling water for 2–3 minutes until *al dente*. Drain with cold water and set aside.

Heat a wok with oil, swirling to coat sides. Stir-fry garlic and green and red bell peppers for 2–3 minutes. Remove from wok.

Add chicken and snow peas to wok and stir-fry for a few minutes until meat turns white. Add a small amount of oil if chicken sticks to side of wok. Add green onions and stir-fry 30 seconds.

Make dressing: Blend together the soy sauce, vinegar, hot chili oil, and crushed red and white pepper.

Return garlic and bell peppers to wok along with the snow peas and noodles. Stir everything together until heated through. Top with crushed nuts and sprigs of parsley.

Serves 4.

Pork

Baked Spareribs with Potatoes, Chinese–Style

Chinese-Style Barbecued Spareribs

Chinese-Style Fisherman's Hash

Chinese-Style Simmered Pork

Ma Po Tofu

Mu Shu Pork

Pineapple Pork Medallions

Pork and Bean Threads with Fuzzy Squash

Roast Pork with Mustard Greens Chow Fun

Spareribs with Black Bean Sauce

Steamed Pork Patty with Chinese Sausage

Szechuan Pork with Bean Threads

hen Chinese chefs speak of meat, they usually start with a discussion on pork. It is used for cooking more than any other kind of meat in China because it is more plentiful than beef, and most Chinese people do not care for the strong taste of lamb. Some cuts of pork contain more fat than other meats, which equates to tenderness and good flavors, ideal for stir-frying, steaming, stewing, deep-frying and claypot cooking. Whenever possible, I use lean cuts of pork, but some recipes require some amount of pork fat in order to maximize flavor (for instance, roast pork). In general, pork has a clean taste, mixes well with other foods, and is easily digestible.

I was raised in a family where we used a great deal of pork. When I think back to my early meals, I see images of hot bowls of pork won ton soup, my Dad's restaurant-roasted, tender pork, steamed pork buns, roast pork spareribs dripping with hoisin sauce glaze, and a smelly but delicious pork hash steamed with salted fish or salted shrimp.

A good example of the pre-dominant use of pork is on the menu of a typical Chinese teahouse where dim sum dumplings dominate the dining ritual of the day. Most of the dumplings and pastries contain some kind of pork. For instance, popular and typical pork-filled dim sum items are pork dumpling, steamed pork bun, spring roll (usually contains slivers of roast pork), steamed pork and mushroom turnovers, stuffed taro (with minced pork and green onions), lotus leaves filled with sticky rice, Chinese pork sausage, minced pork and shrimp, and potstickers.

These pork recipes run the range of traditional Cantonese dishes to newer, creative ideas developed in the modern kitchen.

Baked Spareribs with Potatoes, Chinese Style

This is a recipe from Mom's kitchen. She prepared this often, and I love the idea of combining the potatoes with the spareribs while they are cooking. The potatoes soak up the good marinade flavors.

2–2½ pounds pork spareribs
2 baking potatoes, cut into
   long wedges

MARINADE FOR SPARERIBS
2 cloves minced garlic
⅔ cup hoisin sauce
1 tablespoon red bean curd
   (nom yee) (optional)
¼ cup packed brown sugar
½ cup tomato catsup
2 tablespoons rice wine or
   dry sherry
¼ cup honey
1 tablespoon soy sauce

Remove excess fat from bottom part of spareribs. Place slab of spareribs on a cutting board and cut between bones about ½ inch so marinade soaks through well. Place all marinade ingredients in a large bowl and mix together until well-blended. Place ribs in a shallow pan and spread marinade on both sides, and set for at least 2 hours (overnight is best).

Line a baking pan with aluminum foil and place a baking rack in it. Pour water in baking pan to 1 inch from bottom, but not touching rack. Place spareribs on rack, meaty side up, and bake at 350 degrees for 30 minutes. Turn over spareribs and baste with leftover marinade, add potatoes to the side of the pan, and bake for another 30 minutes. Turn spareribs once again and switch to broil for the last 4–5 minutes (keep an eye on the ribs) until spareribs have a nice glaze and an almost burnt appearance. Remove, cool for 10–15 minutes to ease cutting into individual ribs. Serve with potatoes on the side.

Serves 6 or more.

Chinese–Style Barbecued Spareribs

Select lean spareribs, perhaps back ribs. Spareribs are always great for luncheons, dinners, or picnics. For ease in cleanup, line the bottom of the baking pan with aluminum foil. Simply discard the aluminum foil before washing the pan.

2½–3 pounds pork spareribs (request your butcher to cut the slab of ribs into halves, against the bones)

MARINADE FOR SPARERIBS
½ cup hoisin sauce
½ cup tomato catsup
½ cup rice wine or dry sherry
2 tablespoons soy sauce
3–4 cloves minced garlic
2 tablespoons honey (optional, adds a nice glaze)

Combine the marinade ingredients in a bowl and add the spareribs. Marinate the spareribs for 2–4 hours at least. Overnight is best.

Heat oven to 375 degrees. Remove spareribs from marinade and place them on a rack in a shallow baking pan, filled slightly with water, but not touching the ribs. Roast in the oven for 45–60 minutes. Baste spareribs after 30 minutes with leftover marinade. Cut into individual ribs for serving.

Serves? This is a difficult one to call. The appetite for ribs varies wildly.

Chinese–Style Fisherman's Hash

My father-in-law, Bernard Carver, created this dish as a way of cooking for his fishing buddies, using only one pot. As you may surmise from the name, he's not Chinese. However, it is a dish that lends itself well to cooking in a wok and to the use of Chinese ingredients. The following ingredients are listed per person, and should work for one to six people. Adjust amount according to how vigorously the fishermen must work.

¼ cup milk
1 egg
2 slices white or whole wheat bread, cut into 1-inch squares

In a medium-sized bowl, add milk and egg and mix well. Add bread to the mixture and stir until all sides of the bread are coated, adding more milk if

1 tablespoon vegetable oil
¼ cup onion, thinly sliced
¼ cup diced roast pork,
  Chinese sausage, or other
  sausage or bacon
¼ cup cooked Chinese black
  mushrooms, cut into small
  pieces
dash of black pepper
¼ cup minced green onion

necessary. Set aside.

Heat a wok with oil, swirling to coat sides. Stir-fry onion over medium heat until it becomes translucent. Add meat and mushrooms. Cook until meat is lightly brown (Chinese roast pork and sausage will not change color). Lower heat and add the egg, milk and bread mixture. Stir occasionally until the bread squares start to brown. Add pepper to taste and top with green onion.

Serves 1.

Chinese–Style Simmered Pork

This is a very simple recipe that results in a savory entrée, cooked in its own juices and mild seasoned liquid. If desired, serve with a vegetable such as chopped napa cabbage, cooked along with the pork for the final 10 minutes.

3–3½ pounds pork shoulder
  roast
2 tablespoons vegetable oil
2 tablespoons fresh ginger,
  minced
1 tablespoon garlic, minced
1 cup water
1 cup chicken broth
1 cup green onions, cut into
  1-inch pieces (slap the white
  part gently with the side of a
  cleaver to release flavors)
1 cup rice wine or dry sherry
½ cup soy sauce

Heat a wok or large, heavy skillet with oil, swirling to coat sides. Gently place the roast in the wok and brown the meat on all sides. Add ginger and garlic and cook for 10–15 seconds to brown slightly. Add water, chicken broth, green onion, wine, and soy sauce. Bring to a boil, reduce heat and simmer for 2 hours, or until meat is tender.

Serves 8.

Ma Po Tofu

Legend says that this dish was first created by an old woman for her husband. They lived in a house that stood between a tofu shop and a lamb shop. The old woman often prepared minced lamb and bean curd for the help. Ma Po means "pock-marked old woman's tofu."

---

1 tablespoon vegetable oil
¼ pound lean ground pork
1 heaping teaspoon fresh ginger, minced
4 cloves garlic, minced
3–4 whole hot chili peppers
2 tablespoons soy sauce
1 tablespoon brown bean sauce
½ cup chicken broth
2 teaspoons cornstarch mixed well with 1 tablespoon cold water
1 teaspoon sesame oil
4 cubes fresh soft or medium tofu, cut into 1-inch cubes
¼ teaspoon hot chili oil
2 tablespoons minced green onion

Heat wok with 1 teaspoon oil, swirling to coat sides. Stir-fry the pork over high heat until it turns brown. Remove from wok and drain on paper towels.

Reheat wok with remaining oil. When smoky, add ginger, garlic, and hot chili peppers and cook for 30 seconds. Add the soy sauce and brown bean sauce, and return pork to wok. Add chicken broth, bring to a boil and stir in cornstarch mixture. Add sesame oil and carefully turn in the tofu to cook gently in the sauce for 4–5 minutes. Add hot chili oil and more sesame oil to taste. Top with green onions.

Serves 3–4.

Mu Shu Pork

½ pound lean pork, cut into thin slivers

12 mu shu pancakes: home-made (SEE RECIPE FOR THESE ON PAGE 179) or purchase in specialty market

MARINADE FOR PORK

1 tablespoon rice wine or dry sherry
1 tablespoon soy sauce
1 teaspoon cornstarch

OTHER INGREDIENTS

¼ cup lily stems
¼ cup cloud ear fungus
¼ cup bamboo shoots, shredded
3 tablespoons vegetable oil
3 eggs, slightly beaten
1 tablespoon rice wine or dry sherry
1 teaspoon soy sauce
1 teaspoon sesame oil
3 green onions, cut into 2-inch lengths, and into thin slivers
3 tablespoons vegetable oil
hoisin sauce
sesame oil
thin slivers of green onion

Combine wine, soy sauce, and cornstarch in a small bowl. Add pork and marinate for 20–25 minutes.

Soak lily stems and cloud ear fungus in hot water for 5 minutes. Squeeze out excess water and chop coarsely.

Heat wok with 2 tablespoons vegetable oil, swirling to coat sides. When very hot, scramble the beaten eggs until golden; remove and set aside.

Reheat wok and add the pork, stirring vigorously to separate pieces, and cook over high heat until brown, about 2 minutes. Remove pork and set aside.

Add another tablespoon of oil to the wok. Stir-fry the lily stems, cloud ear fungus, and bamboo shoots over high heat for 2 minutes.

Return the pork to the wok, add the wine, soy sauce, and sesame oil. Return the eggs to the wok, breaking them up into lumps. If desired, season with a little more sesame oil. Transfer to a serving platter. Place the slivers of green onions on a plate. Combine some hoisin sauce and sesame oil on another plate. Open a pancake. Spread hoisin and sesame oil mixture lightly over the center and top with a few slivers of green onion. Spoon 2 tablespoons of filling into the center of the pancake. Fold one end of the pancake over the filling. Fold the other half, like a crepe.

Yield: 12 mu shu pancakes.

Pineapple Pork Medallions

This is sweet and sour pork with a new name. Although this dish is not traditionally Chinese and is often called a tourist's delight, it is a favorite Chinese menu item.

1 pound lean pork, cut into
  1-inch cubes
1 tablespoon soy sauce
⅓ cup cornstarch
⅓ cup flour
2 cups vegetable oil

SWEET AND SOUR SAUCE
1 yellow onion, cut into 1-inch
  cubes
2 stalks celery, cut into ⅛-
  inch thick slivers
7 ounces pineapple chunks
  (or 1 small can), reserve
  juices
½ cup catsup
3 tablespoons brown sugar
1 tablespoon rice or wine
  vinegar
1 cup cold water

OTHER INGREDIENTS
1 green bell pepper (for
  additional color use half red
  and half green pepper)
1 tablespoon cornstarch
  mixed well with 2 tablespoons cold water
2–3 tomatoes, cut into 1-inch
  cubes
¼ cup toasted sesame seeds

Sprinkle soy sauce over pork. Place ⅓ cup cornstarch and flour mixture in a medium-sized bowl. Add a few of the pork cubes to the bowl at a time, and coat each piece.

Heat a wok with 2 cups of oil for deep-frying. Shake excess flour off each piece of pork before frying. Fry pork for 2–3 minutes over high heat, until golden brown. Drain well and set aside.

Heat a wok with no oil. Add onion, celery, pineapple juice, catsup, sugar, vinegar, and water. Bring to boil. Add pineapples and bell peppers. Stir in cornstarch mixture. Add cooked pork and tomatoes to the wok. Cover and simmer for 2–3 minutes until vegetables are cooked and sauce is thickened. Adjust thickness of sauce if necessary. Transfer to serving platter and sprinkle with sesame seeds.

Serves 3–4.

Pork and Bean Threads with Fuzzy Squash

This is a dish that can be served hot or at room temperature, excellent to bring for potluck or to a summer picnic. If fuzzy squash is not available, use zucchini. You may add 1 tablespoon dried shrimps, soaked in hot water for 10 minutes, and drained. This adds a salty tang to this traditional dish. And for more variety, add ½ cup each of sliced carrots and celery.

4 Chinese dried black
  mushrooms
1 fuzzy squash, approximately
  ½ pound
2 ounces dried bean threads
¼ pound lean pork, sliced into
  thin strips
1 teaspoon rice wine or dry
  sherry
½ teaspoon soy sauce
¼ teaspoon cornstarch
1 tablespoon vegetable oil
1 yellow onion, thinly sliced
1 teaspoon fresh ginger,
  minced
½ cup chicken broth
1 teaspoon soy sauce
1 teaspoon cornstarch mixed
  well with ¼ cup liquid from
  soaked mushrooms
2 tablespoons minced green
  onions
dash of white pepper
¼ teaspoon sesame oil

Soak mushrooms in hot water for 10 minutes. Drain and squeeze out excess water. Reserve liquid to add to cornstarch mixture later. Remove and discard stems and slice caps into thin slivers.

Use a potato peeler to remove fuzz, rind, and blemishes from squash. Cut into 2-inch-long matchstick-sized pieces.

Soak bean threads, covered, in hot water for 5 minutes. Drain, cut into 3-inch sections and set aside. Place pork strips in small bowl and add dry sherry, soy sauce, and cornstarch. Mix well.

Heat wok with oil, swirling to coat sides. When smoky, stir-fry the pork for a minute until seared, but not cooked through. Add onion, ginger, black mushrooms, and stir-fry for 2–3 minutes, until onion is translucent. Add bean threads and chicken broth. Cover to cook for 3–4 minutes. Bean threads will cook and absorb most of the liquid in the wok. Add soy sauce and stir in cornstarch mixture and cook until sauce thickens. Top with green onions and white pepper, and drizzle with sesame oil.

Serves 3–4.

Roast Pork with Mustard Greens Chow Fun

Chef Lee Alan Dung and I made up this recipe in Honolulu at the American Institute of Wine & Food's headquarters. Instead of rice noodles, we used rice noodle rolls that we purchased in Honolulu's Chinatown. The rolls were filled with roast pork and dried shrimp, which added good flavors to the dish. Any other green vegetable can be substituted for our favored Chinese mustard greens. If available, use hearts of Chinese mustard greens.

---

4 Chinese dried black mushrooms
3 (approximately 1 pound) strips fresh "fun"—rice noodles, or filled rice rolls available in Asian pastry shops
1 ½ tablespoons vegetable oil
1 yellow onion, thinly sliced
½ cup of Chinese yellow chives, cut into 1-inch pieces (optional)
1 cup roast pork, sliced into 1-inch long pieces
2 cups Chinese or other mustard greens, chopped into 2-inch pieces
1 tablespoon soy sauce
2 teaspoons hoisin sauce
white pepper to taste
sesame oil to taste
1 whole green onion, cut into ½-inch pieces

Soak mushrooms in hot water for 10 minutes. Squeeze out excess water, remove and discard stems, and cut caps into slices. Cut rice noodles into strips to approximately ½ inch wide.

Heat wok with oil, swirling to coat sides. When smoky, add onion, yellow chives, mushrooms, and roast pork. Cook over high heat until fragrant, about 30 seconds. Add mustard greens and cook for another 2–3 minutes. Add noodles, soy sauce, and hoisin sauce, and stir for another minute to mix everything together. Season with white pepper and sesame oil. Top with green onions.

Serves 4

Spareribs with Black Bean Sauce

1½ pounds pork spareribs, cut Chinese-style to 1-inch-sections

BLACK BEAN SAUCE
2 tablespoons fermented black beans, rinsed and drained
2 cloves garlic, minced
1 teaspoon fresh ginger, minced
1 tablespoon soy sauce
1 teaspoon rice wine or dry sherry
½ teaspoon sugar

OTHER INGREDIENTS
1 tablespoon vegetable oil
1 yellow onion, diced into 1-inch pieces
1 cup chicken broth
1 green bell pepper, diced (or ½ red and ½ green bell pepper for extra color)
1 tablespoon cornstarch mixed well with 1 tablespoon cold water

Boil the spareribs in 3 cups of water for 3–4 minutes to get rid of excess fat. Rinse with cold water and set aside.

To prepare black bean sauce, place black beans and garlic in a small bowl, and mash together with end of a cleaver. Stir in ginger, soy sauce, wine, and sugar.

Heat wok with vegetable oil, swirling to coat sides. Stir-fry the onions and spare-ribs over high heat for 2–3 minutes. Add black bean sauce, and stir until all the ribs are coated with the sauce. Add broth and cook over high heat for 1 minute. Lower heat and simmer for 15–20 minutes. Stir in cornstarch mixture and add bell peppers. Simmer for another 2–3 minutes, until bell peppers are cooked and sauce thickens. Add small amount of soy sauce if desired.

Serves 6 as a side dish.

Steamed Pork Patty with Chinese Sausage

This pork hash is another example of traditional Cantonese home-style cooking. Pork is plentiful and inexpensive in China, and is used frequently in the kitchen. If possible, use fresh waterchestnuts. Or, if available, substitute jicama for waterchestnuts.

¾ pound lean ground pork
4 Chinese dried black mushrooms
4 fresh or canned water-chestnuts, chopped coarsely
2 links of Chinese lean sausages (lob cheung)
½ teaspoon fresh ginger, minced
1 thin slice of fresh ginger, 2 by 3 inches, cut into matchstick-sized pieces
1 tablespoon rice wine or dry sherry
2 teaspoons soy sauce
½ teaspoon salt
2 teaspoons cornstarch
1 teaspoon green onion, minced

Soak mushrooms in hot water for 10 minutes. Drain, squeeze out excess water, remove and discard stems, and mince caps.

Place rack in wok, and fill wok with water for steaming. Mix together ground pork, waterchestnuts, black mushrooms, sausage and minced fresh ginger. Place mixture in bowl, and add wine, soy sauce, salt, and cornstarch. Shape the pork patty into a shallow 8-inch plate or pie pan, and top with remaining ginger. Steam over high heat for 20–30 minutes, or until pork is no longer pink. Check the wok every now and then, as more water may be required. If so, add hot water. Sprinkle with green onion before serving.

Serves 3–4.

Szechuan Pork with Bean Threads

2 ounces bean threads
½ pound lean ground pork

MARINADE FOR PORK
2 cloves garlic, minced
1 teaspoon fresh ginger,
  minced
1 tablespoon rice wine or dry
  sherry
1 tablespoon soy sauce

OTHER INGREDIENTS
1 tablespoon vegetable oil
1 cup fresh spinach
½ cup chicken broth
1 teaspoon sesame oil
½ teaspoon white pepper

Soak bean threads in hot water for 5 minutes until soft. Drain well, cut to 3-inch lengths. Set aside.

Combine garlic, ginger, wine, and soy sauce in a medium-sized bowl. Add pork and marinate in the refrigerator for at least 30 minutes.

Heat wok with 1 teaspoon of the vegetable oil. When hot, stir-fry spinach over high heat for 1 minute, adding a small amount of chicken broth. When the spinach is bright green, remove from wok to a platter and cover.

Reheat wok with remaining oil, swirling to coat sides. Stir-fry the pork over high heat for 2–3 minutes. Remove.

Reheat wok, add bean threads and remainder of chicken broth, cover and cook for 3–4 minutes. Stir in cornstarch mixture and continue to cook until sauce thickens. Add more soy sauce if desired. Return cooked pork to wok and mix well. Return spinach to wok and toss lightly. Drizzle with sesame oil and white pepper.

Serves 2–3.

Beef

Asparagus Beef

Beef Stir-Fried with Chinese Broccoli

Beef with Oyster Sauce

Beef with Spinach over Noodles

Beef with Tofu

Chinese-Style Beef Stew

Chinese-Style Pepper Steak

Curry Beef Chow Mein

Mongolian Beef

Oxtail Stew

Oyster Beef Won Ton

Steak Cubes with Fresh Asparagus

Stir-Fried Beef with Bok Choy

Stir-Fried Beef with Snow Peas

Tomato Beef Chow Mein

erhaps in no other area is the contrast in the American and Chinese diet more striking than in the use of beef. When we begin my walking tours of Chinatown, we break the ice by having our guests introduce themselves and share what is their favorite food. I would guess that steak is the second most popular choice, just behind chocolate.

When I was growing up, my parents would occasionally serve beef for dinner. One good-sized steak sliced into bite-sized pieces served our family of seven. My father satisfied our youthful craving for hamburgers by personally grinding some steak for the meat. So it was not surprising when a young beau took me to McDonald's on a rather casual first date, I was so appalled that I refused to eat anything.

Although the Chinese are known as the most omnivorous people on earth, many are indifferent to the consumption of beef. There are numerous cultural reasons for this: Buddhism is a popular religion which emphasizes vegetarianism. The ox is revered as a patient and reliable beast of burden. In many parts of China, there continues to be very little space for the grazing of animals, and most breeds of cattle are not adapted to the hot humid weather that occurs in much of East Asia. Because many Chinese are lactose intolerant, there is almost a total absence of dairy products in their food, and consequently few cattle kept for dairy products.

Fortunately for those who live in the United States where beef is abundant, the Chinese long ago encountered Asian nomads who raised and consumed beef in the grassy regions to the north and west, resulting in some great beef dishes. My husband's most frequently ordered dish when we go out for Chinese food is Mongolian Beef. Regarding my own consumption of beef, I like to follow the Taoist principle that you should "Practice everything in moderation, even moderation."

Flank and top round steaks are recommended for most stir-fry dishes. In some areas, butchers suggest coulotte or teriyaki steak, so ask at your market which is the freshest and the best for your particular need. Beef ought to smell fresh, look reddish, and feel moist. If the beef is off-color, looks gray, or appears dry at the end, choose another piece. At best, buy it fresh from a butcher, not pre-packaged. Use it as soon as possible after purchase, and if you need to store it in the refrigerator, wrap it in plastic first. To insure tenderness, remove all excess fat, slice the meat against the grain, and marinate before cooking.

Asparagus Beef

This is a simple and very popular dish, served over rice

for lunch or dinner as a rice plate.

1 pound flank, coulotte, or
teriyaki steak
1 pound fresh asparagus

MARINADE FOR BEEF
1 tablespoon soy sauce
1 teaspoon minced fresh
ginger
2 tablespoons rice wine or dry
sherry
½ teaspoon sugar
1 teaspoon cornstarch

BLACK BEAN SAUCE
SEE *Master Black Bean Sauce*,
RECIPE ON PAGE 201

OTHER INGREDIENTS
2 teaspoons vegetable oil
1 yellow onion, thinly sliced
¾ cup chicken broth
1 tablespoon cornstarch mixed
with 2 tablespoons cold
water

Combine the soy sauce, ginger, wine, sugar, and cornstarch in a small bowl for marinade. Trim fat from beef; slice against the grain into 1½- by 1-inch pieces. Marinate beef for 10–15 minutes.

Prepare the black bean sauce.

Break off tough part of asparagus at the lower stem. Slice diagonally into thin pieces, leaving the tips intact.

Heat wok. Add 1 teaspoon oil, swirling to coat sides. Stir-fry the asparagus for 1 minute. Remove and set aside. Reheat wok with remaining oil, swirling to coat sides. Stir-fry the onion, beef, and black bean sauce over high heat.

Return asparagus to wok and mix with beef. Add the chicken broth, and bring to a near-boil. Form a well in the center of the wok, stir in cornstarch mixture, and continue to cook until sauce thickens slightly.

Serves 3–4.

Beef Stir–Fried with Chinese Broccoli

This is an all-time favorite. If Chinese broccoli is not available, substitute 2 cups of ordinary market broccoli. If regular broccoli is used, trim the stems and cut diagonally into 1½-inch pieces, leave smaller florets intact, and cut larger ones lengthwise into halves or quarters.

¾ pound flank, round, cuolotte, or top sirloin

MARINADE FOR BEEF
1 tablespoon soy sauce
1 teaspoon fresh ginger, minced
2 teaspoons rice wine or dry sherry
1 teaspoon cornstarch

BLACK BEAN SAUCE
1½ tablespoons fermented black beans
2 cloves garlic, minced
1 teaspoon rice wine or dry sherry
1 teaspoon soy sauce
½ teaspoon sugar

OTHER INGREDIENTS
1 tablespoon vegetable oil
½ teaspoon fresh ginger, minced
2 cups Chinese broccoli, trimmed and cut into 2-inch pieces
1 yellow onion, sliced thinly
¾ cup chicken broth
1 tablespoon cornstarch mixed well with 2 tablespoons cold water
soy sauce, to taste

Trim beef and slice against the grain into thin ½-by-1½-inch pieces. Combine the soy sauce, ginger, wine, and cornstarch in a medium-sized bowl. Place beef in bowl with marinade for 10–15 minutes.

Prepare the black bean sauce: place fermented black beans and garlic in a small bowl, and mash together with the end of a cleaver. Stir in wine, soy sauce, and sugar. Set aside.

Heat wok with 1 teaspoon vegetable oil. Stir-fry minced ginger and broccoli for 2 minutes, add ¼ cup chicken broth. When broccoli becomes bright green, remove from wok and wipe wok clean. Place remaining 2 teaspoons of oil in wok. When smoky, stir-fry beef for 1 minute over high heat, to sear meat. Immediately add onion and black bean sauce and continue to stir-fry.

Return broccoli to wok, and add remaining chicken broth. Bring to a gentle boil, stir in cornstarch mixture. Add additional soy sauce to suit taste.

Serves 4.

Beef with Oyster Sauce

1 pound flank steak, coulotte,
  or top sirloin
1 teaspoon soy sauce
1 teaspoon rice wine or dry
  sherry
1 teaspoon cornstarch

OTHER INGREDIENTS
1 tablespoon vegetable oil
½ yellow onion, thinly sliced
1 teaspoon fresh ginger,
  minced
2 tablespoons oyster sauce
½ cup chicken broth
2 teaspoons cornstarch mixed
  with 1 tablespoon cold water
1 tablespoon green onion,
  minced

Trim beef. Slice against the grain into 2-by-2-inch pieces. Sprinkle with soy sauce, wine, and cornstarch.

Heat wok with oil, swirling to coat sides. Stir-fry onion and ginger until onion turns translucent. Add beef and stir-fry for 30 seconds over high heat. Add oyster sauce and cook over high heat for another 30 seconds. Add chicken broth, and bring to a boil. Form a well in the center of the wok and gently stir in cornstarch mixture and continue to cook until mixture thickens. Top with green onions.

Serves 3–4.

Beef with Spinach over Noodles

¾ pound coulotte, flank, or top
   sirloin steak, sliced against
   the grain into thin, ¾-by-
   1-inch pieces

MARINADE FOR BEEF
1 teaspoon fresh ginger,
   minced
1 tablespoon soy sauce
1 tablespoon rice wine or dry
   sherry

OTHER INGREDIENTS
1 pound fresh Chinese egg
   noodles
2 tablespoons vegetable oil
2 cloves garlic, minced
2 bunches fresh spinach, cut
   into 2-inch pieces
1 tablespoon oyster sauce
½ cup green onion, minced
2 cups beef broth
2 teaspoons cornstarch mixed
   well with 1 tablespoon cold
   water
sprigs of Chinese parsley
   (cilantro) (optional)

Place beef in bowl, add marinade, mix well, and set aside for at least 30 minutes.

Heat 2 quarts of water in a large pot. Stir in noodles and let cook for 5–6 minutes. Remove, and drain in colander. Rinse with cold water, to prevent sticking. Transfer to serving platter and cover to keep warm.

Heat wok with 1 tablespoon vegetable oil, swirling to coat sides. Add garlic and spinach, and stir-fry over high heat for 2–3 minutes until spinach wilts. Transfer to a platter and keep warm.

Reheat wok with remaining oil. Stir-fry beef for 2–3 minutes. Add oyster sauce, green onions, and broth. Bring to a boil, and gradually stir in cornstarch mixture, cooking until sauce thickens slightly. Return noodles to the wok and mix with rest of ingredients. Return spinach to wok and mix lightly. Garnish with Chinese parsley.

Serves 4–5.

Beef with Tofu

Beef with tofu served over rice is a traditional one plate meal. If possible, purchase fresh bean cake in Asian supermarkets, where it is available on large trays or floating in buckets of water.

¾ pound round, flank, or
   coulotte steak

MARINADE FOR BEEF
1 tablespoon soy sauce
1 tablespoon rice wine or dry
   sherry
⅛ teaspoon sugar
sprinkle of cornstarch

OTHER INGREDIENTS
1 tablespoon vegetable oil
½ yellow onion, thinly sliced
2 cloves garlic, minced
1 slice fresh ginger root, cut to
   matchstick-sized pieces
2 dried red chili peppers,
   broken into halves
2 squares of fresh tofu, cut into
   1-inch cubes
1 tablespoon brown bean
   sauce (min see jeung)
⅔ cup chicken broth
2 teaspoons cornstarch mixed
   with 1 tablespoon cold water
½ cup green onion, cut into 1-
   inch pieces
sesame oil to taste
white pepper to taste

Slice beef against the grain into 2-inch strips. Place beef in bowl, add marinade, mix well, and marinate for 30 minutes.

Heat wok. Add vegetable oil, swirling to coat sides. When the wok is very hot, stir-fry the beef for less than 1 minute, until outside is braised. Remove and set aside.

Reheat wok, adding a little more oil only if wok looks very dry. Stir-fry the onion, garlic, and ginger over medium high heat until onion is translucent. Add chili peppers.

Return beef to wok, and stir in tofu and brown bean sauce. Continue to cook over high heat and add chicken broth. Bring to a boil, stir in cornstarch mixture, and continue to cook until sauce thickens slightly. Add green onion and drizzle with sesame oil. Sprinkle with white pepper.

Serves 4.

Chinese-Style Beef Stew

One of the advantages of working in our family restaurant throughout my high school days was occasionally being treated to Dad's Beef Stew. Whenever it was a "special of the day," I would scoop some stew over a bowl of cooked noodles or won ton. So good! Idea: add 2 small potatoes at the same time carrot or turnip is placed in wok. Chinese-style beef stew meat must be asked for—it is the bottom of the flank steak. For a substitute, request the "sirloin tail."

1½ pounds Chinese-style beef stew meat, cut into 1-inch cubes
1–2 tablespoons soy sauce
1 tablespoon vegetable oil
1 yellow onion, thinly sliced
3 tablespoons soy sauce
4 cloves star anise
3 cups beef broth
2 carrots, sliced diagonally into 1-inch pieces or 2 cups of Chinese turnip, cut into 1-inch pieces
1 cup cubed (1 inch) potatoes (optional)
1 tablespoon cornstarch mixed well with 2 tablespoons cold water

Bring a large pot with water to a boil. Add beef and boil for 2–3 minutes to get rid of excess fat. Rinse beef with cold water, place in a bowl and sprinkle with enough soy sauce, to cover pieces of beef, but not to saturate the beef.

Heat wok or heavy skillet with vegetable oil. Braise the beef, add onions, soy sauce, star anise, and broth. Cover and simmer for 1½ hours. During the last half hour, add carrots or turnips. Bring beef stew back to a boil, stir in cornstarch mixture slowly to thicken.

Serves 4–5.

Chinese–Style Pepper Steak

I learned about Texas-style pepper steak in a German restaurant in San Antonio. It was a huge slab of porterhouse topped with peppercorns. Had I used that steak for this recipe, it would have served 10 people! This version is dedicated to all my friends in Texas, where I lived for two memorable years.

1½ pound flank, teriyaki, or coulotte steak

MARINADE FOR BEEF
1 teaspoon fresh ginger, minced
1 tablespoon soy sauce
1 tablespoon hoisin sauce
2 teaspoons Worcestershire sauce
1 teaspoon rice wine or dry sherry

OTHER INGREDIENTS
2 tablespoons vegetable oil
½ yellow onion, thinly sliced
1 whole green bell pepper, cut into thin strips, about 2 inches long
1 heaping teaspoon crushed Szechuan peppercorns
½ cup chicken broth
1 teaspoon cornstarch mixed well with 2 teaspoons cold water

Trim beef and slice against the grain into thin pieces, 1 by 1½ inches. Place marinade ingredients in a medium-sized bowl. Add beef and marinate for at least 30 minutes—the longer, the better.

Heat wok with 1 tablespoon oil, swirling to coat sides. When smoky, add onion and bell peppers and stir-fry for 2–3 minutes, until onion becomes translucent. Transfer vegetables to a platter.

Reheat wok with remaining oil. When the wok is very hot, add beef and peppercorns and cook over high heat to desired doneness, approximately 1–2 minutes. Return onion and bell pepper to wok, add broth, bring to a boil and stir in cornstarch mixture. Continue to cook until sauce thickens slightly.

Serves 4–5.

Curry Beef Chow Mein

The Chinese use soy sauce the same way the Indians use curry, in almost every dish. Here, the combination of curry and beef is excellent, saucy and spicy. Try this with fried noodles or over rice.

1 pound flank, round or coulotte steak

MARINADE FOR BEEF
1 teaspoon soy sauce
1 teaspoon rice wine or dry sherry
1 teaspoon cornstarch

SAUCE
1 heaping tablespoon curry powder, more or less to suit personal taste
1 teaspoon sugar
⅔ cup chicken broth
1 tablespoon soy sauce
1 tablespoon rice wine or dry sherry
1 teaspoon coconut milk (optional, to add richness to sauce)

OTHER INGREDIENTS
2 quarts water
1 pound Chinese egg noodles
4 tablespoons vegetable oil
1 yellow onion, thinly sliced
1 green bell pepper (or half red and half green for added color), cut into narrow 2-inch slices
1 teaspoon cornstarch mixed well with 2 teaspoons cold water

Trim and slice beef against the grain into thin pieces, 1 by 1½ inches. Place marinade ingredients in a medium-sized bowl. Add beef and marinate for 10 or more minutes.

In another bowl, combine the curry powder, sugar, chicken broth, soy sauce, wine, and coconut milk. Set aside. Bring two quarts of water to boil. Stir in noodles for 10 seconds only. Drain in colander; rinse with cold water to prevent noodles from sticking.

Heat a large frying pan with 3 tablespoons oil, swirling to coat the bottom well. When the oil is hot, stir in the noodles, distributing evenly with chopsticks. Brown one side; flip the noodles over and brown the other side. Turn fried noodles out of pan. After noodles cool, place on cutting board and cut into eighths with cleaver or knife.

Heat wok with remaining tablespoon of oil, swirling to coat sides. Stir-fry the onion and bell pepper over medium-high heat for 1–2 minutes, until onion turns translucent. Remove vegetables and set aside.

Reheat wok, adding a little more oil if necessary, and stir-fry beef quickly over high heat, for about 2 minutes, or longer to desired doneness. Return vegetables to wok. Add sauce, and bring to boil; gradually add cornstarch mixture and continue to cook until sauce thickens. Return noodles to wok and mix well.

Serves 4–5.

Mongolian Beef

Mongolian Beef is almost a staple in most Chinese restaurant menus, usually served on top of a bed of deep-fried rice sticks. It is an excellent rice dish (in which case, skip the rice sticks). This simple beef dish is cooked very quickly over high heat, with a small amount of seasoning. This is an example of how Mongolian cowboys cooked their meals over camp fires.

1 pound flank steak or top round, trim the fat

MARINADE FOR BEEF
1 tablespoon soy sauce
2 tablespoons rice wine or dry sherry
1 teaspoon cornstarch

OTHER INGREDIENTS
1 tablespoon vegetable oil
$\frac{1}{4}$ cup fresh Chinese ginger, cut into thin slivers
2–3 whole dried chili peppers
3 whole green onions, cut into 1-inch-long pieces; white parts cut into slivers
2 tablespoons soy sauce
1 tablespoon rice wine or dry sherry
1 teaspoon sugar
$\frac{1}{2}$ cup chicken or beef broth
1 teaspoon cornstarch mixed well with 2 teaspoons water

Trim beef, slice against the grain into paper-thin pieces, 1 by 1$\frac{1}{2}$ inches. Mix marinade ingredients into a bowl and add beef to marinate for 30 minutes or longer.

Heat wok with oil, swirling to coat sides. Add ginger and chili peppers and cook until aromatic and peppers begin to turn black. Discard peppers. While heat is still high and smoky, add beef and green onions, and stir-fry quickly for 2 minutes. Add soy sauce, rice wine or dry sherry, and sugar, continuing to stir-fry for 30 seconds. Stir in chicken or beef broth, bring to a mild boil, and stir in cornstarch mixture.

Serves 2–4.

Oyster Beef Won Ton

Important note: if you're not in the mood to go through the whole process of making won tons, you can omit them from this recipe. Oyster Beef without won tons (or sans won tons as they say in Paris) is super over a bowl of noodles, or thickened and served over rice.

---

40 won tons, prepared ahead of time (SEE *Won Ton Soup* RECIPE PAGE 62)

1 pound flank, coulotte, or teriyaki steak

MARINADE FOR BEEF
2 teaspoons soy sauce
2 teaspoons rice wine or dry sherry
1 teaspoon fresh ginger, minced

OTHER INGREDIENTS
6 cups water
1 tablespoon vegetable oil
2 coin-sized slices fresh ginger
2 cups bok choy or Swiss chard, cut diagonally to 1-inch pieces
2 tablespoons oyster sauce
2–3 green onions, cut to 1-inch pieces
2 cups chicken broth
1 teaspoon soy sauce
2 teaspoons cornstarch mixed well with 1 tablespoon cold water
¼ teaspoon white pepper

Trim beef and slice against the grain into ⅛-inch thick strips. Combine the marinade ingredients in a medium-sized bowl. Add beef and marinate at least 30 minutes.

Boil 6 cups of water in a pot. Add won tons, 6–10 at a time, and cook until they float to the top, about 4 minutes. Place in a colander, rinse with cold water, and set aside.

Place wok over high heat until hot. Add 1 teaspoon oil, swirling to coat sides. Stir-fry ginger and bok choy for 2 minutes. Remove and set aside.

Reheat wok, adding the remaining oil. Sear the beef over high heat for 1 minute. Return the bok choy to the wok and stir-fry for another 2 minutes. Add oyster sauce and green onions. Add chicken broth and a teaspoon soy sauce, and bring to a near-boil. Stir in cornstarch mixture, and cook until soup thickens. To serve, place won tons in individual bowls or serving tureen. Pour beef and bok choy mixture on top. Sprinkle with white pepper.

Serves 6–8.

Oxtail Stew

3 pounds oxtail
4 teaspoons vegetable oil
1 yellow onion, diced
6 cloves garlic, minced
1 teaspoon fresh ginger,
  minced
⅓ cup soy sauce
¼ cup rice wine or dry sherry
3 star anise
2 cups chicken broth
4 russett potatoes, cubed into
  1-inch pieces (sprinkle with
  flour, deep-fry until golden
  brown)
4 carrots, cut into 1-inch
  sections

1 teaspoon cornstarch mixed
  with 2 teaspoons cold water
1 teaspoon hot chili oil
1 teaspoon sesame oil
½ cup green onions, minced
Chinese parsley (cilantro)

Remove joints and excess fat from oxtail. Boil for 5 minutes in water to remove more fat. Drain and set aside.

Heat wok. When smoky, add first 3 teaspoons vegetable oil and brown oxtails for several minutes. Remove oxtails and drain excess fat.

Heat a large (6-quart) heavy-duty (e.g. cast iron) pot with remaining teaspoon of oil. Stir-fry onion until translucent. Transfer oxtail from wok to pot. Add garlic, ginger, soy sauce, wine, and anise. Gradually stir in chicken broth and mix well. Cover and simmer for 3½ hours. Add potatoes and carrots and simmer for an additional 30 minutes. Skim excess fat from top, and stir in cornstarch mixture. Continue to cook until stew thickens. Top with chili and sesame oil, green onion, and Chinese parsley.

Serves 6–8.

Steak Cubes with Fresh Asparagus

1 pound fresh asparagus
1 pound coulotte, teriyaki, or filet mignon steak

MARINADE FOR BEEF
2 teaspoons soy sauce
1 tablespoon rice wine or dry sherry
1 teaspoon fresh ginger, minced

OTHER INGREDIENTS
1 tablespoon vegetable oil
1 yellow onion, thinly sliced
1 heaping tablespoon hoisin sauce
1 teaspoon soy sauce
½ cup beef or chicken broth
1 teaspoon cornstarch mixed well with 2 teaspoons cold water

Bend asparagus spears towards the bottom stem to break naturally. Slice asparagus diagonally into thin 1½-inch pieces.

Trim beef and cut into 1-inch cubes. Combine with soy sauce, wine, and ginger in a medium-sized bowl. Add beef and marinate for at least 30 minutes. Heat wok with 1 teaspoon oil, swirling to coat sides.

Stir-fry the onion and asparagus for 2–3 minutes, until onion turns translucent. Remove to plate and cover.

Reheat wok with remaining oil. Add beef and stir-fry for 2–3 minutes. Add the hoisin sauce and soy sauce. Return vegetables to wok. Add the broth, bring to a boil, and stir in cornstarch mixture until sauce thickens.

Serves 5–6.

Stir-Fried Beef with Bok Choy

This is a flexible recipe. Use your favorite cut of beef, and substitute seasonal vegetables for bok choy. Bok choy is available throughout the year, so it is used in many Chinese recipes.

¾ pound flank, coulotte, or
   sirloin steak

MARINADE FOR BEEF
1 teaspoon soy sauce
2–3 teaspoons rice wine or dry
   sherry
1 teaspoon fresh ginger,
   minced
1 teaspoon sugar
1 teaspoon cornstarch

OTHER INGREDIENTS
1 tablespoon vegetable oil
1 yellow onion, thinly sliced
2 coin-sized pieces of fresh
   ginger
2 cups bok choy (or any other
   Chinese greens or broccoli),
   cut diagonally to 2-inch
   pieces
¾ cup beef or chicken broth
1 teaspoon oyster sauce
2 teaspoons cornstarch mixed
   with 1 tablespoon cold water
1 tablespoon green onions,
   minced

Slice beef against the grain into 1-by-1½-inch strips. Combine the soy sauce, wine, ginger, sugar, and cornstarch in a medium-sized bowl. Add the beef and marinate for 30 minutes.

Heat wok with 1 teaspoon vegetable oil. When the wok is very hot, stir-fry onion, ginger, and vegetables. Remove vegetables and set aside.

Reheat wok with remaining 2 teaspoons oil, swirling to coat sides. Stir-fry the beef quickly over high heat for a minute. Return vegetables to wok. Add broth and oyster sauce. Stir in the cornstarch mixture and continue to cook until sauce thickens slightly. Top with minced green onions.

Serves 2–3.

Stir-Fried Beef with Snow Peas

For the presentation of this dish, spread snow peas attractively around the serving platter and place beef in the center.

1 pound flank steak or top sirloin

MARINADE FOR BEEF
1 tablespoon soy sauce
1 tablespoon rice wine or dry sherry
1 teaspoon minced fresh ginger root
1 teaspoon sugar
1 teaspoon sesame oil
1 teaspoon cornstarch
¼ teaspoon white pepper

OTHER INGREDIENTS
4 teaspoons vegetable oil
½ pound fresh snow peas
2 slices of fresh ginger, cut into matchstick-sized pieces
⅓ cup chicken broth
1 teaspoon oyster sauce
1 teaspoon soy sauce
1 teaspoon cornstarch mixed well with 2 teaspoons cold water
½ teaspoon sesame oil

Trim beef and slice against the grain into thin pieces, approximately ¼-inch thick and 1½ inches long. Mix marinade ingredients, and place beef in bowl to marinate for at least 30 minutes—the longer, the better.

Heat wok with 1 tablespoon oil, swirling to coat sides. Stir-fry snow peas for approximately 1 minute, or until they turn bright green. Remove snow peas and set aside.

Reheat wok with remaining oil, swirling to coat sides. Add ginger and cook for 30 seconds. Add beef and continue to stir-fry over high heat. Return snow peas to wok, add chicken broth, oyster sauce, and soy sauce, and continue to cook for another minute. Bring liquid to a boil, form a well in the center of the wok, and stir in cornstarch mixture. Continue to cook until sauce thickens. Drizzle with sesame oil to serve.

Serves 3–4.

Tomato Beef Chow Mein

A few friends insisted that I include this classic Cantonese favorite, pan-fried noodles with tender beef and fresh tomatoes, and catsup. The catsup part might sound blasphemous, but did you know that catsup is a Chinese word? In Cantonese, "fon cat" = tomato; "jup" = sauce. You can transform this dish into Curry Tomato Beef Chow Mein by simply adding curry powder to suit personal taste, after noodles are returned to wok.

---

1 pound coulotte, teriyaki, or flank steak

MARINADE FOR BEEF
1 tablespoon soy sauce
1 teaspoon rice wine or dry sherry
1 teaspoon fresh ginger, minced

OTHER INGREDIENTS
1 pound Chinese egg noodles
5 tablespoons vegetable oil
1 yellow onion, cut into 1-inch chunks
1 green bell pepper, cut into 1-inch chunks
2–3 tomatoes, cut into wedges
1 teaspoon brown sugar
3–4 tablespoons tomato catsup
2/3 cup beef or chicken broth
1 teaspoon cornstarch with 2 teaspoons cold water

Trim beef and slice against the grain into 1-by-1/8-inch thin pieces. Combine the marinade ingredients in a medium-sized bowl. Add beef and marinate for at least 10 minutes.

Bring 2 quarts of water to a boil in a large pot. Cook noodles for 10 seconds only. Drain and rinse with cold water to prevent noodles from sticking.

Heat a large frying pan with 3 tablespoons oil to coat bottom well. When the oil is hot, stir in the noodles, distributing evenly with chopsticks. Add a small amount of oil to the side of the pan if the noodles stick to the pan. Brown one side. Flip the noodles over, and brown the other side. This process takes approximately 15 minutes. Remove fried brown noodles and set aside. When noodles are cooled, break them apart with your cleaver or knife, into eighths.

Heat wok. Add remaining 2 tablespoons oil. Stir-fry the beef over high heat for a minute, just to sear the meat. Remove beef and set aside.

Add onion and bell peppers to the wok and stir-fry for 2 minutes. Return the beef to the wok, and add tomatoes and brown sugar. Add catsup and broth, and bring to a boil. Stir in cornstarch mixture and cook until sauce thickens. Return noodles to wok and mix until heated through.

Serves 2–3.

Vegetables

Asparagus with Whole Black Mushrooms

Baby Bok Choy with Whole Black Mushrooms

Bean Sprouts Stir-Fry

Braised Asian Eggplant in Spicy Sauce

Chinese Black Mushrooms and Tofu

Classic Tofu Chow Yuk

Fresh Spinach with Fermented Bean Curd

Lo Han Jai—Buddhist Vegetarian Stew

Mom's Steamed Eggs

Simple Chinese Broccoli with Oyster Sauce

Simple Spinach and Garlic Stir-Fry

Spicy Hot Tofu

Stir-fried Chinese Green Vegetables

Stir-Fried Prawns with Long Beans

Stir-Fried Tomatoes and Eggs

Stuffed Black Mushrooms

Stuffed Tofu

Unstuffed Tofu

Tofu with Chicken and Prawns

Triple Mushrooms with Vegetables on a Bed of Bean Thread

Ong Choy (Chinese Spinach) Stir–Fried with Soiybean Sauce

Quick 'n Tasty Lettuce Stir-fry

Vegetarian Potstickers

Wilted Spinach with Bay Shrimp

Vegetables play a major role in the Chinese diet. My childhood memories conjure visions of one, if not more, stir-fried Chinese vegetables at our dinner table every night. Often, they would also appear in our daily soup, or stir-fried with meat, poultry, or fish. My father loved to have what he considered a cold salad—a wedge of iceberg lettuce with hoisin sauce dip. Mother stir-fried the same type of lettuce with a small amount of oil, broth and salt, simple and tasty.

Because green vegetables are easy to grow, less expensive than meat, poultry, or seafood, we eat more of them. Quick stir-frying or blanching are two methods of cooking vegetables. They are usually seasoned with a small amount of salt, and/or soy-based sauces. It is important to cook vegetables properly and quickly, with the end results of perfect flavor and bright color, never overcooked. If Asian vegetables are not easily attainable in your community, substitute with ones that are similar in appearance and flavor, or experiment by using favorite vegetables. Here are a few examples:

bok choy: swiss chard

fuzzy squash: zucchini

Chinese okra: zucchini

Chinese broccoli:

  American broccoli

Chinese taro: potato

Chinese long beans: green beans

water spinach: spinach

waterchestnuts: jicama

We also like to use vegetables that cook slowly, such as Chinese turnips (also known as daikon), taro, and lotus roots. They absorb the combined flavors of the other foods and sauces, creating delicious, home-style dishes.

Tofu, also known as bean cake, is a soybean product that seems to gain popularity constantly. The very diverse tofu is available fresh, packaged, deep-fried, pressed with soy-based flavors, and made into noodle form. Fresh tofu can be kept in the refrigerator for 3–4 days at best, placed in a container with cold water to cover. Change water daily. I mince pressed flavored tofu for Vegetarian Potstickers—it gives the texture and illusion of meat, and helps to hold the other vegetable ingredients together. Because tofu is fairly bland, it picks up on the flavors of the other food and sauces with which it is cooked. Personally, I like to add cubes of tofu to noodle soup.

Asparagus with Whole Black Mushrooms

1 pound fresh asparagus
8 Chinese dried black
  mushrooms
1 tablespoon vegetable oil
2 cloves garlic, minced
1 teaspoon fresh ginger,
  minced
2 tablespoons oyster sauce
½ cup chicken broth
1 teaspoon cornstarch, mixed
  well with 2 teaspoons cold
  water

Break the tough portion of bottom stems off the asparagus and discard. Cut into 1-inch pieces. Soak mushrooms in hot water for 10 minutes until soft. Squeeze out excess water, remove and discard stems, and leave caps whole.

Heat wok with oil, swirling to coat sides. Add garlic and cook over medium high heat approximately 1 minute until golden brown. Add mushrooms and cook for 2 minutes. Add asparagus and oyster sauce and stir-fry another 1–2 minutes. Add chicken broth, bring to a boil, and stir in cornstarch mixture, cooking until sauce thickens.

Serves 2–3.

Baby Bok Choy with Whole Black Mushrooms

2 pounds baby bok choy
24 whole Chinese dried black
  mushrooms
4 teaspoons vegetable oil
1 teaspoon fresh ginger,
  minced
2 tablespoons soy sauce
1 tablespoon oyster sauce
2 tablespoons rice wine or
  dry sherry
1 teaspoon sugar
1 ¼ cup chicken broth
  (includes soaking water
  from mushrooms)
1 teaspoon cornstarch mixed
  well with 2 teaspoons cold
  water
2 cloves garlic, minced
2 teaspoons sesame oil
sprigs of Chinese parsley
  (cilantro)

Trim baby bok choy into bite-sized pieces.

Soak mushrooms in hot water to cover for 10–15 minutes. Squeeze out excess water, remove and discard stems, and leave caps whole. Reserve soaking water.

Heat wok with 1 teaspoon oil. Add ginger and cook for 1 minute until fragrant. Add soy sauce, oyster sauce, wine, sugar and 1 cup of chicken broth. Bring to a boil and add mushrooms. Cover and cook over low heat for 10–12 minutes. Stir in cornstarch mixture and cook until sauce thickens.

While the mushrooms are cooking, heat another wok with 1 tablespoon oil, swirling to coat sides. Add garlic and cook until golden brown. Add baby bok choy and stir-fry over high heat for 3–4 minutes until cooked. Add remaining ¼ cup chicken broth and cook until liquid dissolves.

Transfer bok choy to a serving platter and display attractively with leaves facing outward. Place mushrooms, cap side up, in the middle; drizzle with sesame oil and top with sprigs of Chinese parsley.

Serves 5–6.

Bean Sprouts Stir-Fry

2 teaspoons vegetable oil
2 eggs, beaten
4 cloves garlic, minced
1 cup cooked Chinese-
    style roast pork, minced
2 green onions, cut into
    1-inch lengths
½ cup Chinese yellow
    chives, cut into 1-inch
    lengths (optional)
1 pound fresh bean sprouts
⅓ cup vegetarian or
    chicken broth
1 tablespoon soy sauce
¼ teaspoon white pepper
½ teaspoon sesame oil

Heat wok with 1 teaspoon oil, swirling to coat sides. When smoky, stir-fry egg over high heat, omelet style, and remove. Reheat wok with remaining oil. Add garlic, roast pork, green onion, and Chinese chives (if desired) and stir-fry for 30 seconds. Add the bean sprouts, stir-fry for 1 minute. Add broth and soy sauce, stirring until bean sprouts reduce in bulk. Return egg to wok and mix well. Add white pepper. Drizzle with sesame oil.

Serves 2–3.

Braised Asian Eggplant in Spicy Sauce

¼ pound minced lean pork
1 teaspoon soy sauce
½ teaspoon rice wine or dry
   sherry
2 tablespoons vegetable oil
½ yellow onion, thinly sliced
2 Asian eggplants, medium-
   sized, unpeeled, sliced
   diagonally into thin pieces,
   ¼ by 1½ inches
1 teaspoon fresh ginger,
   minced
4 cloves garlic, minced
2 teaspoons chili paste
   with garlic
1 tablespoon soy sauce
⅓ cup chicken broth
2 teaspoons cornstarch
   mixed well with 1 tablespoon cold water
1 teaspoon rice or white
   vinegar
½ teaspoon hot chili oil
1 tablespoon minced green
   onion
1 teaspoon sesame oil

Place pork in a small bowl and mix with the soy sauce and wine.

Heat wok with vegetable oil until smoky. Quickly stir-fry pork until it changes color. Add onion, eggplant, ginger, and garlic. Stir-fry until eggplant softens, approximately 3 minutes. Add chili paste with garlic, soy sauce, and chicken broth. Bring to a boil and stir in cornstarch mixture. Cook until sauce thickens. Lower heat; add vinegar, hot chili oil, and green onion. Drizzle with sesame oil.

Serves 3–4.

Chinese Black Mushrooms and Tofu

Fresh tofu is creamy white and high in protein. It is usually sold in Chinese food markets, displayed on huge pans. Use high-quality black mushrooms whenever possible—they taste so much better. Serve this dish over rice. Add favorite green vegetables if desired, and for extra color (e.g., broccoli or bok choy).

---

8 Chinese dried black mushrooms
2 tablespoons vegetable oil
1 yellow onion, thinly sliced
2 cloves garlic, minced
1-inch slice fresh ginger, cut into matchstick-sized pieces
6 squares of tofu (approximately 3-inch cubes)
1 teaspoon soy sauce
$\frac{1}{2}$ cup chicken broth
1 teaspoon cornstarch mixed with 2 teaspoons cold water
1 whole green onion, minced
white pepper
$\frac{1}{2}$ teaspoon sesame oil

Soak mushrooms in hot water for 10 minutes. Squeeze out excess water, remove and discard stems, and slice caps into small pieces.

Heat wok with oil, swirling to coat sides. Stir-fry onion, garlic, ginger, and mushrooms for 2–3 minutes, until onion is translucent and garlic and ginger are fragrant. Fold in tofu and stir gently. Add soy sauce and chicken broth. Bring to a near boil and stir in cornstarch mixture. Add green onions, sprinkle with white pepper and drizzle with sesame oil.

Serves 4–5.

Classic Tofu Chow Yuk

This is a simple and healthful dish, especially delicious over a plate of fresh steamed rice.

1 cup lean ground pork

MARINADE FOR PORK
1 teaspoon soy sauce
1 teaspoon rice wine or dry sherry
¼ teaspoon cornstarch

OTHER INGREDIENTS
1 teaspoon vegetable oil
4 cubes firm tofu (approximately
　3-inch squares), cut into
　1½-inch cubes
1 tablespoon brown bean sauce
1 tablespoon soy sauce
½ cup chicken broth
1 teaspoon cornstarch mixed well
　with 1 tablespoon cold water
⅛ teaspoon white pepper
1 green onion cut into 1-inch lengths

Combine soy sauce, wine, and cornstarch in a medium-sized bowl. Add pork and marinate for 30 minutes or longer.

Heat wok with oil, swirling to coat sides. Stir-fry the pork for 30 seconds. Add the tofu, stirring gently. Add brown bean sauce and soy sauce. Stir-fry for 2 minutes. Add chicken broth and bring to a boil. Gradually stir in cornstarch mixture, and continue to cook until sauce thickens. Sprinkle with white pepper, top with green onions, and toss lightly.

Serves 3–4.

Fresh Spinach with Fermented Bean Curd

Fermented bean curd is soaked in spices, wine, salt, and water, and sold in jars. This ingredient is an acquired taste for many people. I grew up eating food with several adopted uses of these pungent, salty bean curds.

1 tablespoon vegetable oil
6 cloves garlic, minced
2 teaspoons fermented bean
　curd (or more to suit taste)
1 pound fresh spinach, cut
　into 2-inch pieces
¼ cup chicken broth
2 teaspoons soy sauce
½ teaspoon sesame oil

Heat wok with oil, swirling to coat sides. Add garlic and cook over medium heat until garlic turns golden. Add fermented bean curd and mix with garlic. Add spinach and chicken broth, and stir-fry for 30 seconds or more, until spinach reduces in bulk and turns bright green. Add soy sauce and drizzle with sesame oil.

Serves 2–3.

Lo Han Jai—Buddhist Vegetarian Stew

Lo Han Jai, also known as "Buddhist Vegetarian Stew," is traditionally served on the first day of the lunar Chinese New Year, to cleanse the body. Since ingredients for Lo Han Jai are not easily available in most food markets, this is a simplified version. Although the list of ingredients appears lengthy, once everything is gathered, the cooking is easy. Traditional Lo Han Jai ingredients include ginkgo nuts, lotus root, dried oysters, lily stems, seaweed hair, fried tofu, and dried bean curd sticks.

8 Chinese dried black mushrooms
½ cup cloud ear fungus
2 tablespoons vegetable oil
½ cup sliced bamboo shoots
8 fresh Chinese waterchestnuts, peeled, quartered
1 whole carrot, cut to julienne strips
2 cups napa cabbage
1 cup vegetarian or chicken broth
2 ounces bean threads
1 cup firm tofu, cut to ½-inch cubes
8 snow peas, strings removed, cut in thin slivers
2 cups fresh bean sprouts
2 tablespoons soy sauce
1 tablespoon cornstarch mixed well with 2 tablespoons cold water
1 teaspoon sesame oil

Soak mushrooms and cloud ear fungus in hot water until soft. Drain and squeeze out excess water. Remove and discard stems, and leave caps whole. Cut cloud ear fungus into small pieces.

Heat wok until smoky. Add vegetable oil. Stir-fry mushrooms, cloud ear fungus, bamboo shoots, waterchestnuts, carrot, and cabbage, and cook for 3–4 minutes over high heat. Add broth and bean threads. Cover and cook for 5 minutes over low heat.

Add tofu, snow peas, bean sprouts, and soy sauce. Cover and simmer for 2 minutes. Stir in cornstarch mixture and continue to cook until sauce thickens. Drizzle with sesame oil.

Serves 6.

Mom's Steamed Eggs

My mother's steamed eggs always come out so custard-clear. I think the secret is in the bowl she uses, a medium-sized Chinese soup bowl, lacquered on the outside with colorful Chinese characters and designs, with a plain white interior. A clear 1½ quart heatproof bowl will do fine. These eggs are delicious served over rice. They even taste good without the Chinese sausage or roast pork.

---

8 Chinese dried black mushrooms
½ cup fresh or frozen peas (optional)
4 eggs beaten
2 cups chicken broth
1 tablespoon rice wine or dry sherry
1 tablespoon soy sauce
1 teaspoon salt
1 link of Chinese sausage (lob cheung) or ½ cup Chinese roast pork, cut into thin slivers
¼ cup green onion, minced

Place mushrooms in a bowl and soak in hot water for 4–5 minutes. Squeeze out excess water, remove and discard stems, and mince caps.

Defrost peas, if frozen, to room temperature. Beat the eggs gently, not to a froth.

In a separate heatproof bowl, combine chicken broth, wine, and soy sauce. Add the eggs carefully, stirring to blend. Stir in salt.

Place steamer rack in wok and add water until it almost reaches rack. Place the bowl containing the eggs on the rack. Add the mushrooms, Chinese sausage or Chinese roast pork, and peas to bowl. Fit lid tightly on wok. Cover and cook at high heat for 20–25 minutes without stirring or lifting wok lid. Sprinkle with soy sauce and minced green onion.

Simple Chinese Broccoli with Oyster Sauce

1 pound fresh Chinese broccoli
3 cups chicken broth
1 tablespoon oyster sauce
1 teaspoon sesame oil

Trim tough stems of broccoli. Fill a medium-sized pot with chicken broth and bring to a boil. Add broccoli. Cover and cook over high heat for 2–3 minutes. Combine the oyster sauce and sesame oil in a small bowl. Drain broccoli and transfer to serving platter, and drizzle with oyster sauce and sesame oil mixture.

Serves 3–4.

Simple Spinach and Garlic Stir-Fry

This recipe takes less than 5 minutes to prepare. If you are in a big hurry, use frozen spinach.

1 bunch fresh spinach, cut into
   2-inch pieces
1 tablespoon vegetable oil
3–4 cloves garlic, minced
½ cup chicken broth

Heat wok with oil, swirling to coat sides. When smoky, add garlic and cook over high heat for 30 seconds until garlic turns golden.

Add spinach and stir-fry for 1 minute. Add chicken broth and continue to stir-fry until spinach wilts but is still green, and the broth is reduced.

Serves 2.

Spicy Hot Tofu

This is similar to a vegetarian style of Ma Po Tofu. The seasonings can be adjusted to taste.

BLACK BEAN SAUCE
1 tablespoon fermented black beans, rinsed and drained
2 cloves garlic, minced
1 teaspoon soy sauce
1 teaspoon rice wine or dry sherry
½ teaspoon sugar

OTHER INGREDIENTS
1 tablespoon vegetable oil
1 teaspoon fresh ginger, minced
2 teaspoons green onion, minced
4 cubes firm tofu (approximately 3-inch squares), cut into 1½-inch cubes
1 tablespoon soybean or hot chili paste
½ cup chicken or vegetarian broth
1 teaspoon cornstarch mixed with 1 teaspoon cold water
chili oil, to taste
Chinese parsley (cilantro)

Prepare the black bean paste: place black beans and garlic in a small bowl and mash together with the end of a cleaver. Mix in soy sauce, wine, and sugar.

Heat wok with oil, swirling to coat sides. Add black bean sauce, ginger, and green onion and stir-fry over high heat.

Immediately add tofu and turn gently. Add soybean or hot chili paste and broth. Cover and cook for 3–4 minutes.

Remove cover, form a well in the center of the wok and stir in cornstarch mixture. Cook until sauce thickens. Remove to serving platter and add chili oil, if desired. Garnish with Chinese parsley.

Serves 2–3.

Stir-Fried Chinese Green Vegetables—Bok Choy

This is a very basic Cantonese way of preparing vegetables. Black mushrooms are added to contribute more flavor and color to the dish. Bok choy is quick to prepare and is a good accompaniment to any Chinese meal.

1 ½ pounds bok choy
4 Chinese dried black mushrooms
2 tablespoons vegetable oil
2 cloves garlic, minced
1 teaspoon minced fresh ginger
1 yellow onion, thinly sliced
1 teaspoon soy sauce
½ cup chicken broth
1 teaspoon cornstarch mixed well with 2 teaspoons cold water
½ teaspoon salt

Rinse bok choy well to remove grit. Drain well, and cut into bite-sized pieces.

Soak mushrooms in hot water for 10 minutes. Drain and squeeze out excess water. Remove and discard stems, and cut caps into thirds.

Heat wok with oil, swirling to coat sides. Add garlic, ginger, and onion and cook for a minute until onion is translucent and garlic and ginger are fragrant. Add mushrooms and stir-fry for 2 minutes. Add bok choy, keep the heat high and toss to mix and cook. Add soy sauce and chicken broth, bring to a boil and stir in cornstarch mixture. Sprinkle with salt and add extra soy sauce to flavor, if desired.

Serves 3–4.

Stir-Fried Prawns with Long Beans

If Chinese long beans are not available, substitute with whole green beans or another favorite vegetable, such as broccoli or asparagus.

⅔ pound medium-sized prawns, peeled, deveined, rinsed, and patted dry with paper towels

1 tablespoon rice wine or dry sherry

1 pound (approximately 2 cups) Chinese long beans, cut into 1½-inch pieces

BLACK BEAN SAUCE
1 tablespoon fermented black beans, rinsed and drained

1 heaping teaspoon garlic, minced

1 teaspoon fresh ginger, minced

1 teaspoon soy sauce

½ teaspoon sugar

OTHER INGREDIENTS
2 tablespoons vegetable oil

1 yellow onion, thinly sliced

¼ cup chicken broth

1 teaspoon cornstarch mixed well with 2 teaspoons cold water

1 green onion, cut into 1-inch lengths

Sprinkle prawns with wine.

Prepare the black bean sauce: place black beans and garlic in a small bowl and mash together with the end of a cleaver. Mix in ginger, soy sauce, and sugar and set aside.

Blanch long beans in boiling water to cover for 20–30 seconds until they begin to turn bright green. Drain and set aside.

Heat wok with oil, swirling to coat sides. When the oil is smoky, stir-fry prawns over high heat for about 10 seconds, until they begin to turn pink. Remove from wok and set aside. Add onion, long beans, and black bean sauce, stirring over high heat. When onion turns translucent, add chicken broth and cover to cook for 2–3 minutes.

Return prawns to wok, stir in cornstarch mixture, and cook until sauce thickens. Stir to blend all seasonings together. Top with green onion.

Serves 3–4.

Stir–Fried Tomatoes and Eggs

This is another reminder of my childhood. My mother prepared this simple dish frequently at the height of the tomato season. For the cholesterol-conscious, use egg whites instead of whole eggs.

1 tablespoon vegetable oil
3 eggs (or 1 egg and 4 egg
   whites)
2 small tomatoes, peeled
   and diced
dash sugar
1 green onion, minced
dash of white or black
   pepper

Heat a wok with oil, swirling to coat sides. Gently pour in eggs and cook over medium heat until they begin to harden. Add tomatoes and stir-fry gently until blended. Add dash of sugar. Add green onion and sprinkle with white pepper.

Serves 2.

Stuffed Black Mushrooms

This is party fare. More time-consuming to prepare than most other recipes in this book, but they are delicious.

20 large Chinese dried black mushrooms

FILLING
⅓ pound lean ground pork
6 fresh prawns, peeled, deveined, rinsed, and minced
1 teaspoon salt
3 fresh or canned waterchestnuts, minced
¼ cup green onion, minced
1 tablespoon soy sauce
½ teaspoon sesame oil
⅛ teaspoon white pepper
1 teaspoon cornstarch
⅓ cup chicken broth and mushroom soaking liquid to equal 1 cup liquid
2 tablespoons vegetable oil
2 tablespoons oyster sauce
dashes of white pepper

OTHER INGREDIENTS
1 small head napa cabbage
¼ teaspoon cornstarch mixed with ¼ teaspoon cold water
1 teaspoon Chinese parsley, minced
1 teaspoon green onion, minced

Soak the black mushrooms in hot water for 10 minutes. Squeeze out excess water, remove and discard stems, and leave caps whole. Set aside ⅔ cup of soaking water to add with chicken broth.

Prepare the filling: chop and mix together the pork, prawns, salt, waterchestnuts, and green onion. Place in a large bowl and mix in soy sauce, sesame oil, white pepper, and cornstarch. Set aside.

Heat up enough chicken broth to cover mushroom caps, and simmer for 10 minutes. Drain, towel-dry, and set aside. Place a dab of cornstarch in each mushroom cap. Fill the caps with a generous, but not overflowing amount of filling.

Heat 1 tablespoon oil in fry pan. Place stuffed mushrooms, filling side down, in the pan and brown for 2 minutes. Add reserved mushroom soaking water, chicken broth, oyster sauce, and white pepper. Cover and cook over medium heat for 5–6 minutes.

While the mushrooms are cooking, heat a wok with a tablespoon of oil, and stir-fry the cabbage leaves gently. Splash with a small amount of chicken broth, cover and steam for 1 minute. Drain and transfer cabbage to line a serving platter. Remove mushrooms carefully and place attractively on top of cabbage.

Mix in cornstarch mixture to pan and stir until sauce thickens. Pour over mushrooms. Drizzle with sesame oil. Top with minced parsley and green onion.

Makes 20.

Stuffed Tofu

These stuffed tofus are pan-fried. Many restaurants prefer to deep-fry them because it requires less time. Either method results in a tasty addition to a meal.

4 fresh squares firm tofu, cut diagonally in half

FILLING FOR TOFU
2 Chinese dried black mushrooms
½ cup lean ground pork
4 medium-sized prawns, raw, deveined, rinsed and patted dry
2 or 3 Chinese waterchestnuts, minced
¼ cup green onion, minced
1 teaspoon soy sauce
¼ teaspoon sesame oil
1 teaspoon cornstarch

OTHER INGREDIENTS
2 tablespoons vegetable oil
oyster sauce
sesame oil
1 teaspoon green onion, minced

Soak mushrooms in warm water for 10 minutes. Squeeze out excess water. Remove and discard stems.

PREPARE FILLING: chop and mix together pork, prawns, mushrooms, waterchestnuts, and onion. Mix in a small bowl, and add the soy sauce, sesame oil, and cornstarch. Set aside.

Cut tofu squares diagonally to form triangles. Carefully cut a slit in each triangle of tofu to form a pocket. Place approximately 1 teaspoon of filling into each pocket until all tofu triangles are filled.

Place a wide frying pan over high heat until hot. Add oil, swirling to coat sides. Carefully place each piece of tofu, filling side down, and fry for 2 or 3 minutes, until light brown. Turn occasionally so that each side cooks. Transfer to serving platter. Sprinkle with oyster sauce, sesame oil, and minced green onions.

Makes 8.

Unstuffed Tofu

This recipe was developed to use leftover filling from the previous recipe, Stuffed Tofu, so this is an appropriate although funny-sounding name given by my sister Sarah.

½ cup leftover filling from *Stuffed Tofu* or *Won Ton* recipe *or:*

⅛ pound lean ground pork

2 medium-sized fresh prawns, peeled, deveined, rinsed, and patted dry with paper towel

2 Chinese dried black mushrooms

2 fresh or canned Chinese waterchestnuts, minced

⅛ cup green onion, minced

⅛ teaspoon sesame oil

½ teaspoon cornstarch

OTHER INGREDIENTS

1 tablespoon vegetable oil

½ cup yellow onion, thinly sliced

2 cloves garlic, minced

2 cubes, (approximately 3 inches), firm tofu cut into 1-inch squares

⅓ cup chicken broth

½ bunch fresh spinach, stems removed, coarsely chopped

1 teaspoon cornstarch mixed well with 2 teaspoons cold water

1 teaspoon oyster sauce

1 teaspoon minced green onion

white pepper to taste

½ teaspoon sesame oil

Soak mushrooms in warm water for 10 minutes. Squeeze out excess water, remove and discard stems.

On a chopping board, mix together all leftover filling from previous recipe for stuffed tofu, or the pork, prawns, mushrooms, waterchestnuts, and minced green onion.

Transfer to a medium-sized bowl and add sesame oil and cornstarch and mix well. Shape into ½-inch balls and press down to flatten into patties.

Heat wok with oil, swirling to coat sides. Stir-fry onion slices and garlic until onion becomes translucent. Add meat patties and cook 2–3 minutes until color changes. Add tofu and stir-fry carefully to avoid breaking up. Add broth and spinach and cook for 1 minute. When broth comes to boil, stir in cornstarch mixture.

Add oyster sauce, top with minced green onion and sprinkle with white pepper. Drizzle with sesame oil.

Serves 2–3.

Tofu with Chicken and Prawns

For extra flavor, add 1 tablespoon fermented bean curd after adding the prawns, if you favor a pungent touch to this Cantonese dish.

8 prawns, peeled, deveined, rinsed and patted dry
1 cup dark or white chicken meat sliced to bite-sized pieces

MARINADE FOR PRAWNS
½ teaspoon fresh ginger, minced
1 teaspoon rice wine or dry sherry
1 teaspoon soy sauce

MARINADE FOR CHICKEN
1 teaspoon garlic, minced
1 teaspoon fresh ginger, minced
1 teaspoon soy sauce
2 teaspoons rice wine or dry sherry

OTHER INGREDIENTS
4 Chinese dried black mushrooms
⅛ cup cloud ear fungus
2 tablespoons vegetable oil
1 yellow onion, thinly sliced
8–10 Chinese snow peas, strings removed
½ cup chicken broth
1 teaspoon cornstarch mixed with 2 teaspoons cold water
1 teaspoon sesame oil
1 tablespoon minced green onion
14 ounces tofu, cut into 1-inch cubes

In a medium-sized bowl mix together garlic, ginger, soy sauce, and wine. Add prawns to this mixture. Combine the marinade ingredients for chicken in another bowl. Add chicken and marinate for at least 30 minutes.

Soak mushrooms and cloud ear fungus in hot water for 10 minutes. Drain excess water and set fungus aside. Remove and discard stems, of mushrooms, and cut caps into thirds.

Chop cloud ear fungus into small pieces.

Heat wok with oil, swirling to coat sides. When smoky, add onion, black mushrooms, cloud ear fungus and chicken. Stir-fry over high heat for 2–3 minutes. Add prawns and stir-fry for another 2–3 minutes until prawns turn pink. Add snow peas and tofu and stir for just 1 minute until snow peas turn bright green. Add chicken broth, bring to a boil, and stir in the cornstarch mixture. Continue to cook until sauce thickens. Drizzle with sesame oil, and top with green onions.

Serves 2–3.

Triple Mushrooms with Vegetables on a Bed of Bean Thread

Chef Lee Alan Dung and I created this recipe in Honolulu. As a guest chef for the American Institute of Wine & Food, I organized a 5-course dinner for 60, but changed the menu after shopping with Lee in Honolulu's Chinatown. We used premium Chinese dried mushrooms along with fresh shiitake and fresh oyster mushrooms. If latter mushrooms are not available, use all dried mushrooms, or some canned straw mushrooms.

12 Chinese dried black mushrooms of uniform size—the higher quality, the better

8 fresh shiitake mushrooms, cut into bite-sized pieces

8 oyster mushrooms, cut into bite-sized pieces

2 tablespoons vegetable oil

1 yellow onion, minced

1 heaping teaspoon garlic, minced

1 red bell pepper, seeds removed, cut in half vertically, then into thin strips

1 yellow bell pepper, seeds removed, cut in half vertically, then into thin strips

1 7-ounce can baby corn (fresh is best, if available)

3 ounces bean threads, soaked in hot water until soft, cut into 2-inch lengths

2 tablespoons soy sauce

1 cup chicken broth

2 teaspoons minced fresh ginger

1 tablespoon oyster sauce

1 tablespoon hoisin sauce

1 tablespoon cornstarch mixed well with 2 tablespoons cold water

1 teaspoon sesame oil

Soak the black mushrooms in hot water for 10 minutes. Squeeze out excess water, remove and discard stems, and leave caps whole.

Heat wok with 1 tablespoon oil, swirling to coat sides. When smoky, add minced onion and garlic, cooking until onion is translucent and garlic is aromatic. Add bell peppers and baby corn, and stir-fry for 1 minute. Add bean threads, 1 tablespoon soy sauce, and ½ cup of the chicken broth. Cover and cook for 2–3 minutes. Shut off heat, but cover wok to keep bean threads warm.

To another wok, add remaining tablespoon of oil. When smoky, add ginger and black mushrooms. Cook for 2 minutes. Add fresh shiitake and oyster mushrooms, remaining tablespoon soy sauce, oyster sauce, and hoisin sauce. Add remaining chicken broth, and bring to a boil. Stir in cornstarch mixture and cook until sauce thickens.

Check bean threads. If they look dry, add a small amount of chicken broth and stir. Transfer bean threads to serving platter. Pour mushrooms on top, arranging decoratively. Drizzle with sesame oil.

Serves 4–5.

Ong Choy (Chinese Spinach) Stir-Fried with Yellow Soybean Sauce

Some of the best Chinese foods are those that are simple to prepare. If Chinese spinach is not available, substitute with any other type of spinach, or lettuce.

1 tablespoon vegetable oil
4 cloves garlic, minced
1 ½ pounds Chinese spinach (ong choy) leaves only (save stems to add to stockpot)
1 tablespoon yellow soy bean sauce (available at most Asian specialty markets)
1 teaspoon soy sauce
½ cup chicken broth

Heat wok with oil, swirling to coat sides.

Cook garlic over medium heat for 1–2 minutes until golden in color. Add ong choy, yellow bean sauce, soy sauce, and chicken broth. Stir-fry over high heat until ong choy softens and broth reduces.

Serves 2–3.

Quick 'n Tasty Lettuce Stir-Fry

If your lettuce has a few bruises or has overstayed its welcome in the refrigerator, bring it back to life with this simple recipe.

1 tablespoon vegetable oil
3 cups coarsely chopped fresh lettuce
⅛ teaspoon salt
½ cup chicken broth
oyster sauce to taste
sesame oil to taste

Heat wok with oil, swirling to coat sides. When smoky, stir-fry lettuce over high heat for a minute. Add salt and chicken broth and stir-fry until lettuce becomes soft, approximately 1 minute.

Wih a slotted spoon, transfer lettuce to a serving platter. Drizzle with oyster sauce and sesame oil.

Serves 2.

Vegetarian Potstickers

4 Chinese dried black
   mushrooms
1 pound potsticker wrappers
   (available at most Asian
   specialty markets)

FILLING
1 cup spinach leaves
½ cup shredded napa
   cabbage
½ cup bamboo shoots,
   daikon, or fresh or canned
   waterchestnuts
½ cup pressed bean curd
⅛ cup cloud ear fungus
1 teaspoon green onion,
   minced
1 teaspoon fresh ginger,
   minced
2 cloves garlic

2 teaspoons soy sauce
1 teaspoon rice wine or dry
   sherry
1 teaspoon cornstarch
½ teaspoon sesame oil
pinch of white pepper

OTHER INGREDIENTS
4 teaspoons vegetable oil
2 cups chicken or vegetarian
   broth

Soak mushrooms in hot water for 10 minutes. Squeeze out excess water. Remove and discard stems and cut caps in thirds.

Chop the filling ingredients together until well blended. A food processor will save time but be careful not to over-chop and pulverize the filling. Place mixture into a large bowl, and add the soy sauce, wine, cornstarch, sesame oil, and white pepper. Refrigerate mixture until ready to use.

To assemble potstickers, spoon 1 tablespoon of the filling into the center of each potsticker wrapper. Fold wrapper over to make a half-circle, and pleat edges firmly together. Set each potsticker upright on a platter, so a flat base is formed.

Heat a skillet, preferably a non-stick type. When the pan is hot, add 1 tablespoon oil. Place the potstickers close to one another in the pan and fry until bottoms begin to brown. Pour enough broth into the pan to cover bottom half of potstickers. Cover and cook over moderate heat for 6–7 minutes, until the water evaporates.

Tip the pan to ease the potstickers out. If necessary, add 1 teaspoon oil around the edges. Turn each potsticker over, brown side up, and place on a serving platter.

Have an assortment of small bowls with hot chili pepper oil, soy sauce, rice vinegar, fermented black bean hot oil (if available) and have guests mix their own dips to suit individual tastes.

Makes approximately 20.

Wilted Spinach with Bay Shrimp

1 tablespoon vegetable oil
½ cup minced yellow onion
1 teaspoon fresh
  ginger, minced
3 cloves garlic, minced
½ pound bay (cocktail) shrimp
2 bunches (approximately 1½
  pounds) spinach, leaves only
⅓ cup chicken broth
1 teaspoon soy sauce
1 teaspoon oyster sauce
1 teaspoon sesame oil

Place wok over high heat. Add oil, swirling to coat sides. Stir-fry the minced onion, ginger, garlic, and shrimp for 20–30 seconds. Remove and set aside.

Reheat wok, stir-fry the spinach until it turns a deep green and begins to wilt. Add chicken broth, soy and oyster sauces and cook until broth reduces; return shrimp to wok and mix with spinach for 1 minute. Drizzle with sesame oil.

Serves 3–4.

Rice and Noodles

Basic Chinese Rice Noodles

Basic Fried Noodle Cake

Basic Mu Shu Pancakes

Basic Steamed Rice

Almond Chicken Chow Mein

Asian Noodles

Beef Fried Rice

Beef with Tender Geens Chow Fun (Rice Noodles)

Braised Noodles

Chicken and Prawns Chow Mein

Cold Bean Thread Salad with Bean Sprouts

Dan Dan Noodles

Pan-Fried Noodles with Assorted Vegetables

Rainbow Fried Rice

Roast Pork Gon Lo Mein

Singapore Noodles

ig fon may ah?" in Cantonese translates to "have you eaten rice yet?" In Chinese, asking this question is a form of greeting, and the same as asking if one has had a meal.

About 80% of the Chinese in America come from the south of China, a major rice-growing area. In northern China, the growing season is too short to produce rice, so they consume more wheat and barley products.

Rice is a food staple considered by most Chinese as the family's main source of nourishment. A typical Chinese breakfast consists of rice congee, "jook," which is a small amount of rice cooked with a large amount of water, savored with ginger, meat, and perhaps thousand-year-old egg, and cooked into a thick soup.

Steamed rice always accompanies other dishes at a meal. Begin with a bowl of rice, top it with gravy-laden stir-fried entrées, delicately seasoned steamed fish, or a pile of vegetables. Traditionally, it is steam-cooked and served plain. Occasionally, it is fried with leftovers. In many restaurants, fried rice has its own section today, and can be quite fancy.

Chinese people tend to prefer white rice because it is an attractive backdrop for the other dishes. Restaurants that cater to the health-conscious serve brown rice because it has more nutritional value and fiber content.

There are many types and brands of rice on the market, but the most common for Chinese cooking is long grain white rice, steamed until it is fluffy. I like aromatic jasmine or chewy basmati rice.

Cornell University in New York found in a study of the Chinese diet that the average adult in China consumes about 20% more calories per pound of body weight than the average American. But comparatively few Chinese have weight problems because they consume less than one-third as much fat as Americans. This diet of rice and vegetables may explain why the Chinese have fewer problems with diseases like osteoporosis and certain forms of cancer.

Noodles

Noodles are considered a complete meal for many people. I like noodles so much, I can eat them for every meal, with a little broth or stir-fried, and perhaps topped with some fresh vegetables or leftovers from the refrigerator. In Italian restaurants I almost always order a pasta dish. Inexpensive and filling at the same time, noodles are a good way to stretch the food budget.

In food markets, noodles are available fresh or dried. It is best to go to a factory to buy them freshly packaged. In the stores, they are usually in one-pound clear bags. The categories of noodles seem endless, made of various types of flour added to water, the most common being wheat or rice flour. Rice noodles are made by crushing rice to form a rice milk, and steaming the liquid to form sheets of white rice noodles for "chow fun." Cellophane noodles or rice stick noodles are also popular stir-fried, used in cold or warm salads, and in soups. Egg is added to give a yellow color to some noodles. Here's a lesson in Chinese: "chow" means "to stir-fry" and "mein" means "noodles," so when you order chow mein, you are asking for stir-fried noodles.

For the noodle recipes that follow, you may choose your favorite basic flour and water noodle or a variety of thin or regular egg noodles.

Noodles are always served in traditional Chinese birthday celebratory meals, as they represent long life. May you have many bowls of long noodles in your life as you try out these recipes.

Basic Chinese Rice Noodles—Bok Fun, for Chow Fun Dishes

Rice noodles are also readily available in most Asian food markets, and not necessarily refrigerated. Used primarily for stir-fry chow fun dishes, in soups, or rolled up with minced shrimp, meat, and green onion. They can be kept at room temperature up to 24 hours, or frozen for up to a week, and are best used fresh.

1 cup unsifted rice flour or cake flour
1 tablespoon wheat starch or cornstarch
2 tablespoons vegetable oil
1¼ cups cold water

In a medium-sized bowl, mix flour and starch together. In another bowl, combine oil and water, and pour it into the flour gradually. Stir mixture until it forms a smooth, lump-free batter.

Heat large wok filled with 2 inches water. Place steamer rack inside the wok. Place a lightly greased 9-inch pie pan on rack. Ladle ¼ cup of batter into lightly greased pie pan. Steam over high heat, covered, for 5 minutes. Allow to cool and remove cooked noodle by gently rolling it up, jelly-roll style. Repeat this process until all rice noodles are made.

Basic Fried Noodle Cake

This is a fried noodle cake to use for chow mein dishes. It can be prepared in advance and reheated when mixed in the wok with the rest of the chow mein ingredients.

1 pound fresh Chinese egg
   noodles
8 cups water
2 tablespoons vegetable oil

Bring 8 cups of water to a rolling boil. Place noodles in pot and stir around for 10 seconds. Drain noodles in a colander and rinse with cold water. Rinsing the noodles prevents them from cooking any further, and from sticking together. Set aside.

Heat a 12-inch frying pan with oil, moving the pan around to distribute the oil. Add noodles to form a pancake. Fry noodles for 5–6 minutes. Check every few minutes to see if noodles are turning brown. Flip and cook other side. Add a small amount of oil to the pan if the noodles stick to the bottom. Cook until bottom side is golden brown. Remove to platter. When the chow mein topping is finished, break up cooked noodles into quarters and place into wok to mix everything together.

Basic Mu Shu Pancakes

2 cups all-purpose, unbleached
  flour
¾ to 1 cup of boiling water

Place the flour in a large mixing bowl. Stir in the boiling water a little at a time. Add enough water to make a lumpy dough. When the dough holds together, turn it out to a floured board, and knead until smooth, approximately 5 minutes. With your hands, roll into a log about 1½ inches thick. Cut the dough into 1½-inch chunks. Roll each chunk into a ball between your palms, and flatten it into a patty. Brush one side of a patty with sesame oil, and align the oiled side with another patty and press together. Roll the two pancakes together with a rolling pin to a 5–6-inch diameter.

Heat a dry skillet or crepe pan, with no oil. When the skillet is hot, put the flattened pair of pancakes in it. When brown specks begin to appear on the bottom, turn the pancakes over. When both sides are lightly specked, remove from heat. Continue this process for all the pancakes. When pancakes are cool enough to handle, carefully separate them, peeling them apart. Place them into a steamer until ready to serve.

Basic Steamed Rice for Four

Texas or California long-grain rice are the most common types served in Chinese restaurants. I enjoy Jasmine rice (from Thailand) and Basmati rice (from India), which require ½ cup more water and up to 10 additional minutes of cooking time. Cooked rice stays warm in the pot for 15–20 minutes. Cooked and cooled rice may be sealed, refrigerated and/or frozen for several days. Excellent for fried rice.

2 cups long grain rice
water

Rice should be rinsed repeatedly and thoroughly before cooking. Place the rice in the pot, and using approximately 4 or 5 cups of water, rub the rice between your hands. Change water and repeat until water is clear. (Initially, the water will be quite milky, due to the residue left from the milling process.)

When the rice water is clear, give it a final rinse and add fresh water to measure 1-inch above the rice level. Bring the pot of rice to a boil, and when visible water begins to evaporate, cover and lower heat to simmer for approximately 15 minutes. Remove lid, and fluff the rice up with chopsticks before serving.

Almond Chicken Chow Mein

This is one of my all-time favorite chow meins. My dad made the best, and I hope you'll like my version. You may wish to use a combination of leftover vegetables instead of just one kind. The crushed almonds add a nice taste sensation.

1 whole (approximately 1 pound) boned and skinned chicken breast
Basic Fried Noodle Cake (SEE RECIPE PAGE 178)

MARINADE FOR CHICKEN
2 teaspoons soy sauce
1 teaspoon rice wine or dry sherry
½ teaspoon sugar
½ teaspoon salt
dash of pepper

OTHER INGREDIENTS
2 tablespoons vegetable oil
1 yellow onion, sliced
1 pound favorite vegetables, e.g., baby bok choy, Chinese cabbage, Chinese broccoli, mustard greens, or snow peas
3–4 Chinese waterchestnuts (fresh preferred), sliced
2 cups fresh bean sprouts
1 cup chicken broth
1 tablespoon soy sauce
1 tablespoon oyster sauce
1 tablespoon cornstarch mixed well with 2 tablespoons cold water
1 cup roasted almonds, ½ kept whole, ½ crushed for topping
1 teaspoon sesame or hot chili-sesame oil
Chinese parsley (cilantro) sprigs

Prepare basic fried noodle cake.

Make marinade by combining 2 teaspoons soy sauce, wine, sugar, salt, and pepper. Combine with chicken in large bowl and marinate at least 30 minutes.

Heat wok with oil, swirling to coat sides. When smoky, stir-fry chicken until meat turns white and braises. Remove to platter.

Reheat wok, adding a small amount of oil if necessary. Stir-fry onion and vegetables for a few minutes until they are brighter in color. Add waterchestnuts and bean sprouts and stir-fry for 1 minute.

Return chicken to wok, mix well, add chicken broth and bring to a near boil. Add soy and oyster sauces, and stir in cornstarch mixture. Toss in whole roasted almonds. Drizzle with sesame or hot-chili-sesame oil.

Return noodle cake to wok, mix everything together, adjust sauce if desired. Transfer to serving platter, sprinkle with crushed almonds, and top with Chinese parsley.

Serves 4.

Asian Noodles

When you visit Maui, Hawaii, please drop by and say hello to my friend, chef Mark Ellman, owner of Avalon Restaurant in Lahaina. His food is creative and delicious, and it's a fun and whimsical place to eat. I have adapted one of his recipes for the Chinese kitchen. The only change I made was to use Chinese noodles instead of linguine, but the choice is yours. Add fresh chili pepper to taste while cooking, if desired. Mahalo, Mark!

½ pound fresh Chinese noodles, cooked in advance, rinsed with cold water to prevent sticking, kept warm
6 Chinese dried black mushrooms
1 teaspoon olive oil
1 teaspoon sesame oil
1 teaspoon fresh ginger, chopped
1 teaspoon garlic, chopped
1 teaspoon yellow onion (Maui onion if available), chopped
2 teaspoons Chinese parsley (cilantro), minced
2 teaspoons fresh basil, julienne strips
2 teaspoons fresh mint, julienne strips
1 teaspoon fermented black beans, rinsed
2 teaspoons green onion, minced
4 live clams (Manila preferred)
1 ounce fresh ahi (tuna) or similar fish, cut into ½-inch cubes
4 fresh prawns, peeled and deveined
4 sea scallops, cut into halves, or 8 whole bay scallops
4 ounces fresh tomatoes, peeled, seeded, chopped fine
2 ounces unsalted butter
1 ounce grated parmesan cheese
2 additional tablespoons fresh basil, cut in julienne strips

Soak mushrooms in hot water 10 minutes, squeeze out excess water, remove and discard stems, and slice caps into thin pieces.

Heat wok with olive and sesame oil over medium heat. Add ginger, garlic, yellow onion, Chinese parsley, basil, mint, black beans, and green onion, and stir-fry for 1 minute. Add clams, ahi, prawns, sea scallops, and mushrooms, and stir-fry for 2 minutes. Add tomatoes and butter and stir and mix until seafood is cooked and clams open. Add parmesan cheese and remaining basil and blend together. Serve over Chinese noodles.

Serves 2.

Beef Fried Rice

½ pound flank steak (or any
   type of good beef)
3 tablespoons vegetable oil
2 eggs or 3 egg whites
¼ cup chopped celery
3 cups cooked, cold rice
2 tablespoons soy sauce
½ cup minced green onions
1 cup fresh or frozen green
   peas, thawed
1 cup shredded lettuce
½ teaspoon white pepper
1 teaspoon sesame oil
additional soy sauce to taste

Trim beef and slice into thin pieces, 1
by 1½ inches. Sprinkle with a small
amount of soy sauce and cornstarch.

Heat wok with 1 tablespoon oil,
swirling to coat sides. Fry eggs or egg
whites omelet-style. Remove and set
aside.

Reheat wok with remaining tablespoon of oil. When the wok is hot,
stir-fry the beef and celery for 1
minute. Remove and set aside.

Reheat wok and add another teaspoon of oil if the wok looks dry. Stir-
fry the rice, moving it around the wok
constantly, for 2–3 minutes. Add soy
sauce and continue to stir-fry.

Return beef and celery to wok and
mix well over medium heat. Add
green onions, green peas, and lettuce
and stir-fry for another 1–2 minutes
until everything is well blended.

Return eggs to wok and break up into
smaller pieces. Add white pepper.
Sprinkle with sesame oil and additional soy sauce to taste.

Serves 4–5.

Beef with Tender Greens Chow Fun
(Rice Noodles)

This is a classic Cantonese lunch favorite. Chow fun rice noodles are available in most Asian supermarkets in the refrigerated section, or fresh in pastry and noodle shops. Swiss chard can be used as a substitute for bok choy, the Chinese greens.

¾ pound flank, coulotte, or top
   sirloin

MARINADE FOR BEEF
1 tablespoon soy sauce
1 tablespoon rice wine or dry
   sherry
1 teaspoon fresh ginger, minced

OTHER INGREDIENTS
1 tablespoon vegetable oil
1 teaspoon fresh ginger, minced
1 yellow onion, thinly sliced
2 cups tender greens (bok choy
   or baby bok choy), trimmed
   and cut diagonally into 1½-inch
   pieces
4 strips of "fun" (rice noodles) into
   1-by-1½-inch strips
1 teaspoon soy sauce
2 cups bean sprouts
white pepper to taste
chili pepper oil (optional)
1 green onion, sliced into 1-inch
   pieces
Chinese parsley (cilantro) to
   garnish (optional)

Trim fat from beef, cutting against the grain into 1½-by-2-inch pieces. Combine the marinade ingredients in a medium bowl, add beef, and set aside.

Heat wok. Add 2 teaspoons oil, swirling to coat sides. Stir-fry ginger, onion, and bok choy for 2–3 minutes, until onion turns translucent and bok choy leaves begin to turn bright green. Remove vegetables and set aside.

Reheat wok with remaining oil. Add the rice noodles and stir-fry constantly to prevent sticking. Add the beef and soy sauce, and stir in the bean sprouts. Keep stir-frying for 2 minutes, or longer to preferred doneness.

Return vegetable mixture to wok and mix well. Season with white pepper and more soy sauce, to taste. Mix in a dash of chili oil, the green onion, and top with parsley, if desired.

Braised Noodles

If dried shrimp is not available, leave out, or substitute with ½ cup bay (cocktail) shrimp. This will alter the flavor considerably, but it will still be good.

¾ pound cooked Chinese
  egg noodles
⅓ pound lean pork, cut into
  1½-inch strips

MARINADE FOR PORK
½ teaspoon soy sauce
dash of cornstarch
½ teaspoon rice wine or dry
  sherry

OTHER INGREDIENTS
6 Chinese dried black
  mushrooms
½ cup cloud ear fungus
1 tablespoon vegetable oil
¼ cup fresh ginger, minced
1 tablespoon dried shrimp
2 whole green onions, cut
  into 1-inch lengths, white
  and green parts
1½ cup chicken broth
2 tablespoons soy sauce
1 teaspoon sesame oil
½ teaspoon salt
½ teaspoon white pepper

Mix marinade ingredients in bowl and marinate pork for at least 30 minutes. In separate bowls, soak black mushrooms and cloud ear fungus in hot water to cover, for about 10 minutes. Squeeze excess water from mushrooms, remove and discard stems, and slice caps into thin pieces. Drain cloud ear fungus, and chop coarsely.

Heat wok with oil, swirling to coat sides. When smoky, stir-fry the pork until it changes color. Add ginger, mushrooms, cloud ear fungus, and dried shrimp (or fresh cocktail shrimp) and stir-fry for 2–3 minutes. Add green onions and cook another 30 seconds. Add chicken broth and bring to a gentle boil. Add cooked noodles and mix well. Add soy sauce and sesame oil, salt, and white pepper, cover and simmer for 3–4 minutes. Add more soy sauce to suit personal taste.

Serves 2–3.

Chicken and Prawns Chow Mein

Chow mein is a typical and popular Chinese lunch item. It is easier to prepare than most people think. Many vegetables can substitute for those in this recipe and your favorite seafood can also be added.

½ chicken breast, boned, skinned, sliced to bite-sized pieces
Basic Noodle Cake (SEE RECIPE PAGE 178)

MARINADE
1 teaspoon soy sauce
2 teaspoons rice wine or dry sherry
1 teaspoon fresh ginger, minced
¼ teaspoon cornstarch

OTHER INGREDIENTS
8 Chinese dried black mushrooms
3 tablespoons vegetable oil
1 yellow onion, thinly sliced
1 cup roast pork (if pork is not desired, increase amount of chicken or prawns)
8 prawns, peeled, deveined, rinsed and patted dry
1 pound baby bok choy
2 cups bean sprouts
8 snow peas, strings removed
1 tablespoon oyster sauce
1 cup chicken broth
2 teaspoons cornstarch mixed with 2 teaspoons cold water
1 tablespoon green onion, minced
Chinese parsley (cilantro) sprigs

Make marinade by combining soy sauce, wine, ginger, and cornstarch in a small bowl. Add chicken and marinate for at least 30 minutes.

Soak mushrooms in hot water for 10 minutes. Squeeze out excess water, remove stems, and leave caps whole.

Heat wok with oil, swirling to coat sides. Sear the chicken over high heat for 2 minutes to seal in marinade. Remove and set aside.

Reheat wok, stir-fry onion, mushrooms, pork, and prawns for 2 minutes until onion is translucent and prawns turn pink. Add bok choy, bean sprouts, snow peas, oyster sauce, and chicken broth. Continue cooking over high heat.

Return chicken to wok. Stir in cornstarch mixture. Break up noodle cake into 4–5 pieces. Add to wok and mix well with rest of ingredients. Top with green onion and Chinese parsley.

Serves 3–4.

Cold Bean Thread Salad with Bean Sprouts

This salad can be topped with crushed roasted peanuts and sprigs of Chinese parsley.

---

2 ounces bean threads
4 cups fresh bean sprouts
1 whole green onion, cut into
  1½-inch lengths, then into
  very thin strips
1 cup Chinese yellow chives,
  cut into 1½-inch lengths
4 tablespoons rice or white
  vinegar
1 teaspoon light soy sauce
2 teaspoons sesame oil

Soak bean threads in hot water until soft, approximately 5 minutes. Cut into 3-inch lengths.

Blanch bean sprouts for just about 1 minute to cook. Drain immediately and pat dry with paper towels. Place bean threads in large bowl or shallow baking pan. Top with bean sprouts, green onion and chives. Mix together the rice vinegar, soy sauce, and sesame oil, and pour on top, and blend everything together. Taste and add more vinegar if desired. Serve warm, or cover to refrigerate and serve cold.

Serves 2–3.

Dan Dan Noodles

Soybean paste, chili paste with garlic, and preserved turnip are readily available in most markets specializing in Asian foods. There are no substitutes. This can be made as spicy as you want by adjusting the amount of chili paste with garlic. My favorite brand of chili paste with garlic is Lan Chi.

---

1 pound fresh Chinese egg noodles

SAUCE
2 teaspoons chili paste with garlic
2 teaspoons green onion, minced
2 teaspoons minced preserved
   turnip (optional)
1 teaspoon fresh ginger, minced
1 teaspoon sesame paste
1 teaspoon rice wine or dry sherry

OTHER INGREDIENTS
1 tablespoon vegetable oil
¼ pound lean ground pork
2 teaspoons brown bean paste
   (min see jeung)
1 cup chicken broth
1 teaspoon cornstarch mixed well
   with 1 teaspoon cold water
½ cup green onion, minced
1 teaspoon sesame oil

Heat 2 quarts of water in a pot; stir in noodles and cook for 2–3 minutes. Remove and drain in a colander. Rinse with cold water to prevent sticking. Set aside.

Combine chili paste, green onion, preserved turnip, ginger, sesame paste, and wine in a small bowl. Set aside.

Heat wok with 1 tablespoon vegetable oil, swirling to coat all sides. Stir-fry pork and brown bean paste over high heat for 2–3 minutes. Add the sauce, and continue to stir-fry for 1–2 minutes. Add chicken broth, bring to a boil and stir in cornstarch mixture. Place pre-cooked noodles in individual serving bowls. Pour sauce over noodles. Sprinkle with green onions, and drizzle with additional sesame oil.

Serves 3–4.

Pan-Fried Noodles with Assorted Vegetables

Basic Noodle Cake (SEE RECIPE PAGE 178)
8 Chinese dried black mushrooms
2 tablespoons vegetable oil
1 yellow onion, thinly sliced
2 slices fresh ginger, approximately 1 by 2 inches, sliced thinly into matchstick-sized pieces
½ cup cloud ear fungus
½ cup green onion, minced, or Chinese chives (gow choy)
1 pound total of assorted seasonal green vegetables of your choice, cut to bite-sized pieces: e.g., bok choy, baby bok choy, long beans, mustard greens, Chinese turnip, Chinese cabbage, Asian okra, broccoli
12 snow peas, strings removed
6 fresh or canned waterchestnuts, thinly sliced
1 cup chicken or vegetarian broth
1 tablespoon soy sauce
1 tablespoon oyster sauce
dash of white pepper
1 tablespoon cornstarch mixed well with 1 tablespoon cold water
½ teaspoon sesame oil
Chinese parsley for garnish

Prepare basic noodle cake.

Soak mushrooms in hot water for 10 minutes. Squeeze out excess water, remove and discard stems, leave caps whole.

Heat wok with oil, swirling to coat sides. Stir-fry onion, ginger, mushrooms, cloud ear fungus, and green onion or chives for 2 minutes. Add remaining vegetables and cook for 2–3 minutes. Add broth, soy sauce, oyster sauce, and pepper. Bring to a boil and stir in cornstarch mixture. Cook until sauce thickens.

Return noodles to wok and mix everything together. Drizzle in sesame oil, and top with sprigs of Chinese parsley.

Serves 3–4.

Rainbow Fried Rice

Leftover rice is preferred in preparing fried rice because it is not as sticky as fresh rice. Adding eggs near the end of the cooking gives extra moisture to this colorful dish.

---

3 Chinese dried black mushrooms
2 teaspoons vegetable oil
½ yellow onion, minced
1 cup of or combination of diced
  Chinese-style roast pork, cooked
  ham, Chinese sausage, minced
  prawns (raw or cooked) or
  scallops, cooked chicken, or any
  leftover meat
4 cups cold, cooked long-grain rice
1 tablespoon soy sauce
2 eggs or 3 egg whites, beaten
½ cup fresh or frozen green peas
2 cups lettuce, finely shredded
½ cup green onion, minced
1 teaspoon sesame oil
white pepper

Soak mushrooms in hot water 10 minutes. Squeeze out excess water, remove and discard stems, and mince caps.

Heat wok with oil, swirling to coat sides. Stir-fry the onion and mushrooms until onion turns translucent. Add choice of meat or seafood and stir-fry over high heat for 2 minutes. Add rice and soy sauce and cook over high heat for another 2 minutes, mixing well. Add eggs and cook for another minute. Add peas and lettuce and continue to stir until lettuce cooks. Add additional soy sauce to taste, top with green onion, sesame oil, and a sprinkle of white pepper.

Serves 5–6.

Roast Pork Gon Lo Mein

Sometimes I prefer lo mein to chow mein. Lo mein is similar to chow mein, without the additional step of pan-frying the noodles with oil.

1 pound fresh Chinese egg
   noodles
1 tablespoon vegetable oil
⅔ pound Chinese-style roast
   pork, cut to bite-sized pieces
½ yellow onion, thinly sliced
2 cups bok choy, cut to 1-inch
   pieces
1 cup chicken broth
1 tablespoon cornstarch mixed
   well with 1 tablespoon cold
   water
¼ cup soy sauce
1 cup bean sprouts
1 tablespoon sesame oil
½ cup green onions, minced
white pepper to taste

Place noodles in large pot filled with 6 cups of boiling water. Cook for 2 minutes. Drain in colander; rinse with cold water and set aside.

Heat a wok with oil, swirling to coat sides. Stir-fry the roast pork over high heat for 2 minutes and remove.

Reheat wok and cook until onion is translucent—add bok choy and cook with onion for an additional minute. Add chicken broth and bring to a boil. Stir in cornstarch mixture and continue to cook until sauce thickens.

Return noodles to wok, add soy sauce and mix well. Return roast pork and add bean sprouts. Sprinkle in sesame oil and top with green onions. If desired, shake a little white pepper over noodles.

Serves 4–5.

Singapore Noodles

This is a delicious hot or warm dish, loaded with good flavors. Adjust amount of curry according to taste.

8 ounces bean threads (cellophane noodles)
6 Chinese dried black mushrooms
2 tablespoons vegetable oil
2 eggs or 3 egg whites, beaten
1 yellow onion, thinly sliced
¼ cup celery, minced
¼ cup bamboo shoots, minced
½ green or red bell pepper, sliced into thin strips
1 cup cooked chicken, cut into matchstick-sized strips
1 cup bay (cocktail) shrimp
1 tablespoon soy sauce
1½ cups chicken broth
1 tablespoon curry powder (or more to taste)
¼ cup green onion, minced
1 teaspoon sesame oil
1 teaspoon hot chili oil

Remove outer wrappers from bean threads, keep binding on. Soak in boiling water until bean threads are firm as rubber bands. Use scissors or a sharp cleaver to cut the bean threads into 3-inch pieces. Discard binding. Drain bean threads well, and set aside.

Soak the mushrooms for 3–4 minutes in hot water. Remove and discard stems, and slice mushroom caps into thin pieces.

Heat a wok with 1 tablespoon oil, swirling to coat sides. Fry eggs omelet-style and remove to plate.

Reheat wok, adding a little more oil only if necessary. Add yellow onion slices and stir-fry until onion is translucent. Add celery, bamboo shoots, bell pepper, and mushrooms and continue to stir-fry, mixing well. Add the chicken and shrimp and stir-fry to heat through. Add soy sauce and stir-fry another minute. Transfer to warm platter.

Reheat wok. Add chicken broth and curry, and bring to boil. Add bean threads and cook until most of the liquid in wok is absorbed.

Return cooked ingredients to wok and mix with bean threads. Transfer to serving platter, sprinkle with minced green onions, sesame oil, and hot chili oil.

Serves 4–5.

Basic Oils, Sauces, and Dips

A Sauce for All Seasons

Basic Brown Sauce

Basic Deep-Fry Batter

Chef Peter Merriman's Peanut Dipping Sauce

Fermented Black Bean and Hot Chili Oil

Fresh Ginger and Vinegar Dip

Garlic and Hot Chili Sauce

Garlic and Soy Sauce Dip

Ginger, Soy, and Green Onion Sauce

Hot Chili Pepper Oil

Hot Mustard, Hot Chili Oil, and Soy Sauce Dip

Hot and Spicy Sauce

Hot Pepper Oil

Master Black Bean Sauce

Master Hot and Spicy Sauce

Oyster Sauce

Simple Sweet and Sour Dip

Soy Sauce and Oil Dressing for Fish

Soy Sauce and Sesame Oil Dressing

Soy Sauce and Vinegar Dressing

Sweet 'n Sour Plum Sauce

Sweet and Sour Sauce

There are so many sauces and dips in the food markets today, that many busy cooks probably don't want to bother to make them from scratch. But one big advantage in making your own is that you can be creative and experiment, adjusting mixtures and ingredients to suit your tastes. As a word of encouragement, most of the recipes for the sauces and dips in this section are quick and simple, and can be made on the same day that the dishes which call for them are prepared. Be bold and versatile, mix and match. As an example, we recently took a black bean sauce from a stir-fry dish, mixed it with hot oil and used it as a dip for potstickers—bingo! It was a wonderful surprise.

In restaurants, a typical table setting includes a small lazy susan in the center which holds soy sauce, salt and pepper, and chili sauce. At more elaborate restaurants, in addition to the above-mentioned, we find containers of different types of soy sauces, such as light and regular, and possibly vinegar.

In your home, set out a variety of oils and sauces for your guests to mix and match their own dips. We use many kinds of oils, add ginger, garlic, mustard, fermented black beans, to create a series of sauces and dips that we hope will be a fine addition to your dining pleasure.

A Sauce for All Seasons

A great dipping sauce, recommended for almost any deep-fried chicken, fish, vegetable dish, or fried won ton and egg (spring) rolls.

¼ cup white sugar
½ cup cold water
½ cup rice vinegar
2 tablespoons fish sauce (nam pla, available at most Asian specialty stores)
2 teaspoons ground red chili peppers
½ cup shredded carrot
⅓ cup chopped roasted peanuts

Combine sugar and water in a small saucepan and bring to a near-boil. Lower heat and simmer for 10–15 minutes until sugar dissolves. Stir in vinegar, fish sauce, and chili peppers. Place in serving bowl and refrigerate until ready to use. Top with carrots and peanuts before serving.

Makes 2 cups.

Basic Brown Sauce

2 tablespoons oyster sauce
2 teaspoons brown sugar
dash of white pepper
1 teaspoon sesame oil
1 cup chicken broth
2 tablespoons rice wine or dry sherry
1 tablespoon cornstarch mixed well with 2 tablespoons cold water

Mix together first 6 ingredients in a small saucepan. Bring to a gentle boil, turn off heat, and stir in cornstarch mixture until sauce thickens. If sauce is too thick, add additional broth; if too thin, add a little more cornstarch mixture.

Makes 1 ½ cups.

Basic Deep-Fry Batter

This is an easy recipe that I learned at Dad and Mom's restaurant many years ago. It makes a crisp, yet somewhat light covering for spring rolls, chicken, fish, vegetables, and practically any food you choose to deep-fry.

1 cup cornstarch
1 cup all purpose flour
1 cup cold water
1 egg
1 teaspoon baking powder

Mix together all the batter ingredients in a medium-sized bowl. Blend to pancake-batter consistency. Refrigerate for 20 minutes to set. Stir before using.

Makes 3 cups.

Chef Peter Merriman's Peanut Dipping Sauce

I love this peanut dipping sauce so much, I asked Chef Sandy Barr of Merriman's Restaurant in Waimea, Big Island of Hawaii, to share it with my readers. It is superb with grilled chicken, fish, and even duck. Say hello to owner Peter Merriman and Chef Sandy when you're in Waimea!

1 tablespoon shallots or onion, chopped
2–3 teaspoons vegetable oil
¼ cup chopped basil
6 ounces creamy peanut butter
¼ cup lemon juice
¼ cup soy sauce
½ tablespoon Chinese-style chili paste
5 ounces water
¼ cup firmly packed brown sugar

Sauté shallots or onion in oil until transparent. Add basil and mix thoroughly. Add peanut butter, lemon juice, soy sauce, and cook 3 minutes over low-medium heat while stirring. Add water and sugar, and cover pan and cook for 10 minutes, stirring frequently. Serve warm in dipping bowl.

Makes ½ cup.

Fermented Black Bean and Hot Chili Oil

½ cup vegetable oil
¼ cup fermented black beans
1 tablespoon chopped red
 chili peppers

Rinse fermented black beans and drain well. Place beans in a small bowl and mash beans to a pulp with cleaver end. Heat a tablespoon of vegetable oil in a small saucepan. Roast the chopped chilis in the oil for about 30 seconds. Add the crushed black beans and remaining oil. Remove immediately from heat. Serve at room temperature or cold.

Makes ¾ cup.

Fresh Ginger and Vinegar Dip

Try with dim sum dumplings.

½ cup rice or white
 vinegar
¼ cup fresh ginger root,
 sliced into thin slivers

Mix the ingredients together in a small bowl.

Makes ½ cup.

Garlic and Hot Chili Sauce

Good over fried chicken.

⅓ cup peanut or vegetable
 oil
3 cloves garlic, minced
3 dried red chili peppers,
 finely chopped
2 teaspoons white sugar
⅓ cup soy sauce
1 tablespoon rice vinegar
2 teaspoons sesame oil

Heat oil in a small saucepan. Remove from heat and add all the remaining ingredients in order listed. Stir to blend well. Set aside to cool.

Makes 1 cup.

Garlic and Soy Sauce Dip

Excellent with dim sum dumplings, as a dressing for cold or warm lo mein noodles, or for steamed chicken or fish. Use this as a topping sauce for Chinese Fish Fry.

2 tablespoons soy sauce
1 tablespoon rice vinegar
½ teaspoon sesame oil
⅛ teaspoon sugar
2 teaspoons garlic, finely
  minced

Mix all ingredients together in a small bowl. Set aside for 30 minutes. Serve at room temperature.

Makes ¼ cup.

Ginger, Soy, and Green Onion Sauce

Especially good for cold or warm chicken.

2 tablespoons soy sauce
1 tablespoon fresh ginger,
  finely minced
2 tablespoons green onions,
  thinly sliced (use both green
  and white parts)
3 tablespoons chicken broth
¼ teaspoon sugar
1 teaspoon sesame oil

Combine all ingredients in a medium-sized bowl and mix well. Adjust the amount of soy sauce and sesame oil to suit taste.

Makes ⅓ cup.

Hot Chili Pepper Oil

2 green onions
½ cup fresh ginger root,
  coarsely chopped
1 cup vegetable or corn oil
¼ cup dried red chili pepper
  flakes

Mash the white part of the green onions to release flavors, and cut the green part into 2 inch pieces. Cut the ginger root into small pieces. Heat oil in a small saucepan, add green onions and ginger and cook for 2 minutes over medium heat until green onion wilts. Remove from heat, and set aside for 10 minutes. Discard green onions and ginger. Place dried red chili pepper flakes in a medium-sized bowl. Transfer oil to this bowl and cover. After several hours (or overnight) strain oil, label, and store in bottle or jar.

Makes 1 cup.

Hot Mustard, Hot Chili Oil, and Hot Sauce Dips

Excellent with deep-fried prawns, dim sum, and noodles.

¼ cup dried hot mustard
  powder
3 tablespoons cold water
½ cup soy sauce
¼ teaspoon hot chili oil (adjust
to suit personal taste)

Place mustard powder in a small bowl and add cold water. Mix to smooth consistency, adding more water or mustard as necessary. Place mustard, soy sauce, and hot chili oil in small bowls, side by side for guests to mix together.

Makes ¾ cup.

Hot and Spicy Sauce

This sauce is good over hot noodles, fried chicken, or prawns.

¾ cup water
2 tablespoons soy sauce
2 tablespoons hoisin sauce
2 tablespoons rice wine or sake
½ teaspoon cornstarch mixed
   with 1 teaspoon cold water
1 teaspoon brown sugar
¾ teaspoon hot chili powder
   (adjust to suit personal taste)
sesame oil

Bring water to a boil in small saucepan. Add soy sauce, hoisin sauce, and rice wine or sake. Lower heat and mix in cornstarch, brown sugar, and hot chili powder. Simmer for 2–3 minutes. Drizzle with sesame oil. Serve warm or cold.

Makes ¾ cup

Hot Pepper Oil

1 cup vegetable or corn oil
⅓ cup black peppercorns
   (whole)

Bring oil to high heat in a small pot. Add peppercorns and remove from heat. Set aside for 5 minutes. Strain and discard peppercorns. When oil cools, label and store in a glass bottle or jar.

Makes 1 cup.

Master Black Bean Sauce

Use as base for many stir-fry dishes: prawns, clams, asparagus beef, chicken, almost everything.

1 heaping tablespoon fermented
  black beans
2–3 cloves garlic, minced
1 tablespoon soy sauce
2 teaspoons rice wine or dry
  sherry
½ teaspoon sugar
1 teaspoon hot chili pepper oil
  (optional)

Rinse fermented black beans and drain well. Place black beans and garlic in a small bowl and mash together to a pulp with end of cleaver. Stir in soy sauce, dry sherry, sugar, and hot chili pepper oil (if desired), and blend well.

Makes ¼ cup.

Master Hot and Spicy Sauce

Excellent over cold or hot noodles. Usually cooked with minced ground pork, shrimp, or beef.

1 tablespoon minced garlic
1 tablespoon minced ginger
1 tablespoon hot bean sauce
  (availaible in Asian markets, no
  substitute)
2 cups chicken broth
¼ teaspoon white pepper
1 tablespoon rice wine or dry
  sherry
1 tablespoon soy sauce
1 tablespoon minced green onions
1 tablespoon cornstarch mixed
  well with 2 tablespoons cold
  water

Add ingredients to saucepan in order listed and bring to a gentle boil. Stir in cornstarch mixture. Adjust to desired consistency by adding more cornstarch if too thin.

Makes 2½ cups.

Oyster Sauce

3 tablespoons oyster sauce
1 tablespoon soy sauce
2 tablespoons peanut or
  vegetable oil
2 tablespoons chicken broth
1 tablespoon minced green
  onion

Mix above ingredients in a small bowl until blended well. Use as sauce for cooked cold chicken.

Makes ½ cup.

Simple Sweet and Sour Dip

¾ cup chicken broth
2 cloves garlic, finely minced
1 teaspoon fresh ginger root,
  finely minced
½ cup brown sugar
½ cup rice vinegar or red wine
  vinegar
1 tablespoon tomato catsup
1 tablespoon cornstarch mixed
  with 2 tablespoons cold
  water

Heat all ingredients except for cornstarch in a small saucepan over high heat. When sauce begins to boil, reduce heat and stir in cornstarch mixture, a little at a time, until slightly thickened. Adjust consistency as needed, add more water if dip looks like a gravy, or a small amount of cornstarch if dip is too thin.

Makes 1 ½ cups.

Soy Sauce and Oil Dressing

Good drizzled over freshly steamed fish.

¼ cup soy sauce
2 tablespoons peanut oil
1 teaspoon sugar
1 teaspoon salt
1 heaping teaspoon minced
  green onion

Blend all ingredients in a small saucepan and heat. Add green onions. Prepare just as fish is being steamed.

Makes approximately ⅓ cup.

Soy Sauce and Sesame Oil Dressing

Pour over steamed fish, cold chicken or pork.

½ cup soy sauce
2 teaspoons sesame oil
1 teaspoon green onion, finely
  minced

Blend soy sauce and sesame oil together in a small bowl. Mix in green onion.

Makes ½ cup.

Soy Sauce and Vinegar Dressing

Great over cold or blanched vegetables.

1 tablespoon brown or
  white sugar
¼ cup soy sauce
¼ cup rice, wine, or white
  vinegar
1 teaspoon minced ginger
3 tablespoons peanut oil
2–3 drops of sesame oil

Mix together sugar, soy sauce, vinegar, and ginger in a small bowl. Stir in peanut oil and sesame oil and blend well.

Makes ½ cup.

Sweet 'n Sour Plum Sauce

This sauce is great with any fried appetizer. It may be refrigerated, covered, for several weeks. The plum sauce used in this recipe may be purchased readily in Chinese specialty shops or in supermarkets that carry Asian food specialties.

15 ounces (or one large can) crushed pineapple
½ cup sugar
¾ cup rice or white vinegar
¾ cup water
2 tablespoons cornstarch mixed with 2 tablespoons water
1 cup plum sauce

Heat pineapple, sugar, vinegar, and water in a saucepan. Bring to a boil and stir in cornstarch mixture until sauce thickens. Cool for 10–15 minutes. Gently stir in plum sauce. Serve at room temperature or cold.

Makes 4 cups.

Sweet 'n Sour Sauce

Good with sweet 'n sour pork, minced vegetables or as a sauce for fried won ton.

1 cup cold water
7 ounces (or one small can) pineapple chunks (reserve pineapple juice)
1 yellow onion, cut into 1-inch chunks
1 cup celery, sliced diagonally into thin slivers
½ cup tomato catsup
3 tablespoons brown sugar
1 tablespoon rice or white vinegar
1 tablespoon cornstarch mixed well with 2 tablespoons cold water

Bring water and pineapple juice to boil in a saucepan. Add onion and celery and cook until onion is translucent. Reduce heat, add catsup, sugar, vinegar, and pineapple chunks. Add in cornstarch mixture and stir until sauce thickens well.

Makes 3 cups.

What to Drink with Chinese Food

Of Chinese Banquets, Sparkling Cider, Whiskey, Tea and Beer

When I was young, my parents took me along to many Chinese banquets to celebrate weddings, major anniversaries, birthdays, and family association festivities. These elaborate parties were always held in spacious, multi-level traditional Chinese restaurants. The grandiose dining rooms, accommodating hundreds of people, filled quickly with chatty, boisterous party revelers. Each table was clothed in red, with cleverly folded matching napkins, and seating for ten to twelve.

As soon as people were settled, the food came quickly and endlessly—we usually shared at least ten courses with strangers. I seldom knew or remembered anyone but my family around the table. With a nudge from my mother or father, I greeted "aunts" and "uncles" that I saw only at these functions. I would sit quietly, seen and not heard, and eat food I was slightly familiar with, usually starting with a soup of whole wintermelon, shark's fin or birds' nest, followed by large plates filled with cashew chicken, a steamed fish, whole baby squabs, sometimes a Peking-type duck—a seemingly enormous amount of meat—which reminded me of food from previous formal dinner occasions. I peek into the mirror of my memories and see green bottles of sparkling cider and small bottles of cognac or other whiskey at the center of each round table, with a Chinese bowl filled with ice cubes. The teapot came later, but was largely ignored. The tea cups had another use, which we'll mention soon.

I looked forward to clinking some ice in my glass for sparkling cider, a special treat. It was always fun, although it felt funny, to have ice cubes hit my nose. Some of the adults, especially the men, sipped on a terrible-smelling liquor that flowed out of a small brown bottle, and into their tea cups or water glasses. A few of the women would mix a small amount into their glasses of cider. They seemed to have a better time after that. When dinner was over, another interesting event happened—there was a mad rush for the leftover food to be packed up in white take-out cartons, and someone always tucked the almost-empty bottle of liquor into a bag.

Banquets today are similar to ones I went to in the mid-1950s and '60s. In some cases, the menu has not improved. The cognac or bottle of whiskey continues to grace the center of the tables. For many Chinese, no formal banquet is complete without whiskey. In fact, I observed that some men at the banquet table drank whiskey like water.

Tea is still the most popular beverage at dim sum teahouses and Asian restaurants, and is served throughout the day in Chinese communities. In many traditional Chinese homes, a steaming pot of tea is prepared in advance and offered as soon as guests arrive in one's home. Just like going into a wine cellar to choose a special bottle for guests, a superior tea is picked for special occasions. Tea is very refreshing on its own, and perhaps that is why afternoon teas are so popular throughout the world. Two widely-consumed teas are a fragrant jasmine and a variety of oolong teas, and in today's market, there are many herbal teas and even a dieter's tea. Try various teas to determine which ones please your palate.

For hundreds of years, tea was used as medicine. Modern science indicates that tea may aid in the digestive process, lower blood pressure, strengthen teeth, bones, and the immune system, and prevent some forms of cancer. Tea takes a back seat to cider and whiskey, but it makes good health sense to finish the usually rich and heavy banquet food with a soothing tea, to assist in clearing the system.

How about beer? At a recent dim sum luncheon, every one at our table of ten ordered Tsing Tao beer. The cold beer was a perfect accompaniment for the steamed dumplings, stir-fried vegetables, and noodle dishes. Beer is especially good with hot and spicy dishes, and deep-fried food. Many traditional Chinese people hold strong objections to drinking cold beverages with hot food, as they believe it may create an imbalance in one's system to mix hot liquids with cold.

Of Wine and Chinese Food

In the course of completing this cookbook, my husband and I were involved in a number of wine and Chinese food pairings. We agree that the pairings were the most amusing and fun-filled aspects of working on the book. We invited different friends to our various dinners, cooking some of the same dishes but trying a wide range of wines and champagnes. We simply enjoy each other's company, love to eat and drink together, and I requested that they give open and honest evaluations. I am far from being an authority on pairing Chinese food and wine. My personal conclusions? After all is said and done, if the wine blends well in your mouth, if it tastes good with your meal, and the cost of the wine fits your budget, that is what matters. If you like a red wine with fish, forget the notion that red wine only goes with beef and white wine goes with seafood. Be adventurous and try a variety of wines with food—you may be pleasantly surprised to discover new textures, sensations, and flavors. For years, I always drank Chardonnay, Cabernet Sauvignon, or Merlot with Chinese food. Recently, I learned that Gewürztraminer, Sauvignon Blanc, and Rieslings actually go better with certain Chinese dishes, and so the education continues.

The task of pairing wine with Chinese food may be made complex because so many of our dishes have a combination of sweet, sour, salty, and spicy sauces, *and* we often combine meat or seafood with poultry and vegetables. We also serve several dishes at one sitting, unlike ordering a pasta, seafood, or meat entrée. We were very grateful to be able to share time with wine makers, true wine professionals, to learn a few helpful hints. A highly recommended book on matching food and wine is *Red Wine with Fish,* by Joshua Wesson and David Rosengarten.

On one particularly warm spring day, we drove to Sonoma County, to cook with our friend Ron Mangini, of Viansa Winery. I developed new recipes for the book, and Ron and I came up with this nifty idea to try Viansa's wines with my finished products. We cooked up a storm in the winery's kitchen, chopping with our cleavers to the beat of good ol' rock and roll music, sipping on fine wine. Sam and Vicki Sebastiani, the owners of Viansa Winery and Italian Marketplace, paid a surprise visit to the kitchen to help pair a selection of their wines with my food. I discovered from Sam that his Viansa Barbera Blanc and Chardonnay were equally tasty with Vegetarian Chow Mein, and that Sauvignon Blanc goes well with a host of Chinese flavors, such as a Spicy Whole Tiger Prawns, and earthy Black Mushrooms stir-fried with Chicken and Spinach.

At an in-home food and wine pairing, I cooked an eight-course dinner, and poured Roederer Estate Brut Sparkling Wine, J Sparkling Wine, Chandon Brut, and Cordorniu Brut exclusively throughout the meal. Champagne and sparkling wine complement most Chinese food, and are no longer restricted to toasting someone's good fortune. There is no doubt that champagne and caviar continues to reign as a perfect combination, but we thoroughly enjoyed champagne with course after course of a Chinese meal. We started the evening sipping a small amount of each champagne and sparkling wine, to compare notes on their uniqueness. In order to be diplomatic, let us just say that there were no negative comments on any of the four we chose. Our appetizers of Spring Rolls and Fried Tiger Prawns were tasted with and without dips, to compare the depth and detraction or attraction of the champagne. In both cases, the mild hot mustard and soy dip did not jeopardize the flavorful bubbles. In particular, we were pleased with champagne and a mildly sweet and sour Medallions of Pork dish, as well as with Mustard Greens and Pork Strips in a black bean sauce. They were especially compatible with entrees of Clams in Black Bean Sauce and Buddhist Vegetarian Stew. The champagne was good with Potstickers, as long as we kept the strong chili-based dip to a minimum. The conclusion was that as long as sauces were not overbearing or too spicy, champagne or sparkling wine goes well with every dish.

At a second Chinese food and wine pairing, I poured Rodney Strong Charlotte's Home Vineyard Sauvignon Blanc, and our party of eight agreed it was a good wine for the first courses of crisp Spring Rolls and My Dad's Sweet Rice Spring Rolls. We stayed with the Sauvignon Blanc and introduced Davis Bynum's Fumé Blanc for a Chinese parsley-infused Chinese Chicken Salad and the Potstickers (which did not go over very well with the champagne). Even drenched with hot chili sauce, the potstickers found good company with the sauvignon and fumé blancs. Although champagne and wine were offered with a light soup of Fuzzy Squash, Shiitake Mushrooms and Tofu, the general consensus was to leave the soup alone and enjoy it on its own merit. Sonoma County's Duckhorn Merlot, a personal favorite, became a group favorite when we paired it with Chinese-style Pepper Steak. Davis Bynum's Merlot also scored high with this beef dish. La Crema Pinot Noir was engaging with a whole steamed trout, and the pinot noir found no fault paired with Clams with Black Bean Sauce, which was also good with sauvignon blanc. A happy discovery was made, that fish goes well with both red and white wine. New to us, and a surprising finish to this dinner was Stone's Ginger Flavored Currant Wine, produced in England. It was a big hit drizzled over ice cream, or as a drink over ice with a thin slice of orange. The next evening, I used some of it as a marinade for a sassy Ginger Beef.

One evening I took off my apron and retreated to the magnificent Mandarin Restaurant at Ghirardelli Square in San Francisco. My good friend, owner Julian Mao, put together a menu for our party of nine. Among the diners were two wine professionals, David Cordtz and Doug Grant, and wine collector extraordinaires Bob Baker and Marcie Bunker. The rest of the group were food and wine lovers, so the company was perfect. Our conversation centered naturally on what wines pair best with Chinese food.

We started with a fragrant, dry, semi-fruity Rodney Strong '91 Gewürztraminer, pairing it with mild-tasting Vegetarian Potstickers and Vegetarian Rolls. It was very good; however, the addition of hot chili oil dip and vinegar made the wine taste even better—the dip enhanced the fruitiness of the wine, and was well liked by the majority of the group. Our favorites were a Buena Vista Pinot Noir that was paired with Beggar's Chicken. We especially liked the fact that the Pinot Noir drew out the delicate ginger flavor of the chicken. This wine received unanimous nods when tasted with Tea Smoked Duck, a "match made in heaven," according to one happy wine collector.

As we worked through the banquet courses, we started to mix and match some of the wines with the various foods on the table. Soon, the topic of beer and champagne came up, and the final consensus was this: whereas certain wines undoubtedly pair beautifully with certain foods, there is no set rule. For instance, the Szechuan Prawns were good with Sauvignon Blanc and Gewürztraminer, but a cold beer or a glass of champagne or sparkling wine might be just what is needed to cut the spiciness of the sauce.

Close to press time, we had one more dinner party, this time to address the issue of Gewürztraminer, touted by many wine purveyors as the wine that goes best with Chinese food. We poured Gewürztraminer from award-winning wines produced by Rodney Strong, Rapidan River Vineyards (from Leon, Virginia), and Davis Bynum. The spiciness, floral, fruitiness, and refreshing qualities inherent in most Gewürztraminer blend well with many of the entrées, especially those with a dash of boldness and hot spice. Topping the list were Firecracker Prawns, Chinese Style Roast Pork, Mongolian Beef, Kung Pao Prawns, and Kung Pao Chicken. *Note:* the last two were perfect with Chardonnay.

We in the San Francisco Bay Area are very spoiled, with Sonoma and Napa Counties located so close to home, and countless other fine wineries in the region. Sonoma County alone has almost 200 wineries, while Napa County is not far behind with over 150 wineries. In addition, wineries flourish in areas throughout the country and all over the world. Check your local newspapers' food and wine sections for upcoming wine tastings, spirited wine auctions, cooking classes given by famous chefs at food and wine seminars, and a host of other special food- and wine-related events.

To recap, the Chinese food that was mentioned above, plus a few other suggestions, are placed into categories with wine that we tasted as follows:

Appetizers and Savories
Potstickers—Sauvignon Blanc, Fumé Blanc

Spring Rolls—Champagne or Sparkling Wine, Sauvignon Blanc

My Dad's Sweet Rice Spring Rolls—Sauvignon Blanc

Vegetables
Vegetarian Chow Mein—Barbera Blanc, Chardonnay

Buddhist Vegetarian Stew—Champagne or Sparkling Wine

Stuffed Tofu—Chardonnay

Vegetarian Potstickers—a dry Gewürztraminer

Seafood
Firecracker Prawns—Sauvignon Blanc, Gewürztraminer

Fried Tiger Prawns—Champagne or Sparkling Wine,
'83 Cabernet Sauvignon, Barbera Blanc

Clams in Black Bean Sauce—Champagne or Sparkling Wine, Pinot Noir

Whole Steamed Trout—Pinot Noir

Kung Pao Prawns—Gewürztraminer, Chardonnay, Zinfandel

Chicken

Black Mushrooms with Chicken and Spinach—Sauvignon Blanc

Chinese Chicken Salad—Fumé Blanc

Kung Pao Prawns—Chardonnay, Gewürztraminer, Beer

Beggar's Chicken—Pinot Noir

Pork

Medallions of Pork—Barbera Blanc, Muscat Cannelli,
Champagne or Sparkling Wine

Mustard Greens and Pork Strips—Champagne or Sparkling Wine, Pinot Noir

Chinese-Style Roast Pork—Gewürztraminer

Beef

Chinese-Style Pepper Steak—Cabernet Sauvignon, Duckhorn Merlot

Mongolian Beef—Gewürztraminer, Barbera Blanc, Sauvignon Blanc, Pinot Noir

Ginger Beef—Use Stone's Ginger Flavor Currant Wine for Marinade

Index